10/07
29.95

ASK MONTY

ASK MONTY

THE 150 MOST COMMON
HORSE PROBLEMS SOLVED

Monty Roberts

Illustrations by Jean Abernethy

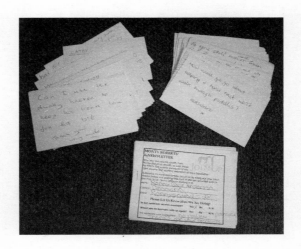

headline

First published in 2007 by
HEADLINE PUBLISHING GROUP

1

Cataloguing in Publication Data is available from the British Library

ISBN 978 0 7553 1722 6

Designed by Ben Cracknell Studios

Typeset in Myriad and Scala by Avon DataSet Ltd,
Bidford on Avon, Warwickshire

Printed and bound in Great Britain by
Clays Ltd, St Ives plc

Headline's policy is to use papers that are natural, renewable and recyclable products and
made from wood grown in sustainable forests. The logging and manufacturing processes
are expected to conform to the environmental regulations of the country of origin.

HEADLINE PUBLISHING GROUP
An Hachette Livre UK Company
338 Euston Road
London NW1 3BH

www.headline.co.uk
www.hodderheadline.com

DEDICATION

This book shall hereby be dedicated to those millions of eyes that I have looked into over the signing stand . . . the eyes of the 12-year-old and of those in their twenties, thirties and even eighties. I dedicate this book to the eyes that looked to me for answers, answers that would assist them in making their time with their horse more enjoyable.

Many people assisted me greatly in the creation of this book: at Headline Publishing Val Hudson and Wendy McCance made it happen, but I am sure everyone would agree that it is the questioning public who earn the full dedication of this effort. It is my sincere hope that every inquiring person will be able to pull from these pages assistance to follow my message of dealing with our horses without violence.

This is my opportunity to thank the more than fifteen million people who have read my books, the more than one million people who have seen me in demonstrations, and the countless who have communicated through emails or watched me in a video. The world of working with horses is dramatically moving away from violence, and it is you and your questioning minds who are responsible for making that happen.

Your questions urge me onward to seek meaningful answers. Your inquiries encourage me to continue my mission to discover more and more ways to communicate with our wonderful animals and to be more efficient in our efforts to educate them. Without your support, I feel I might have retired some time ago. With your enthusiasm, I now can see no retirement on my horizon. Thanks to each and every one of you for the deep interest you have shown.

Monty Roberts

CONTENTS

INTRODUCTION

The individual most responsible for this book is not my wife Pat, who helped me with a lot of typing, editing and organizing, or Giulia Orth, who did the bulk of the typing. Nor is it my daughter Debbie, who did endless hours of work on the computer while we were on the road and gathered the bulk of the questions that I have answered here. It is especially *not me*. *Most* responsible for the creation of this book are those of *you* who asked the tens of thousands of questions from which I chose.

You are the 'doers' in this industry, seeking answers to improve your understanding of, and relationship with, the horses we have come to love. Many people know by now that my life's goal is to leave the world a better place than I found it, for horses and for people too. You know that I cannot do it by myself. Each of you will realize that if we are to succeed in becoming better partners with our horses, it will take an army of individuals who care. You can be part of that army.

There is a movement on this earth of ours to understand horses better and to treat them in a far more reasonable way than we have in the past. I congratulate those who seek information by asking questions. Through this act they are living up to their responsibility to learn as much as they can about the horses they admire. I accept my part of this same responsibility by doing my best to answer these questions.

Before I began work on this book, I had very little idea of how educational it was to answer questions. It requires one to reach into the recesses of one's memory, to replay the mental video of experiences from one's past and to extract from them effective solutions to the challenges met every day while training horses. It is a great challenge to me to word my answers in such a way so as to paint the most understandable picture possible. It is my hope that the reader will be able to put my recommendations into practice. The horses need clear messages, so it is my intention to offer the clearest possible solutions.

I enjoyed this experience, and it is my hope that you will enjoy delving into the answers. We have had domesticated horses on this earth for approximately eight thousand years and, until I came along, it seems there was an unwritten rule that no one questioned the authority of experienced horsemen. Most readers of this book will be able to remember times when they have been told emphatically by a professional horseman, 'Just do what I tell you, and don't ask any questions.' With this mindset, our knowledge of the horse's mind virtually stood still. We did things almost exactly the same for those full eight thousand years. While tradition can be a valuable reminder to respect the past, it can also be an impediment to progress. People starting out in any discipline have the right to question those more experienced, and in my opinion the experienced horseperson is under an obligation to answer those questions.

Throughout those centuries, the central foundation of horsemanship has been tradition. While there are many disciplines, such as architecture and art, where tradition is pervasive, horsemanship stands solidly at the top of the list. Its tradition, as we know from stone carvings, happens to be one of violence and force. It became traditional to break horses with violence, and we have to assume that came about because it 'worked'.

Manned flight, by contrast, is a relatively new discipline on earth, and had no tradition as people attempted to take to the air. At the beginning of the twentieth century, the Wright Brothers successfully conducted the first powered flight at the beach at Kitty Hawk. It was a very modest accomplishment, but opened the minds of bright young people around the world. Unencumbered by tradition, within seventy years we were walking on the moon.

In my demonstrations, I often speculate on what the horse is thinking. I speak for the horse, so that the audience can get a feel for what I believe is going on in the horse's mind. People enjoy this dialogue, and I believe it is because we have a genuine interest in discovering the thoughts of our horses.

You might ask what qualifies me to produce a question-and-answer book, and I suppose I would answer by stating that almost seventy years of experience in dealing with horses qualifies me more than most people. Horses have been wonderful to me, and I believe that eight World Championships in the show ring further qualify me. Each of these was in the world of Western competition, but I also trained more than four hundred international stakes winners in racing. I have worked with horses in more than twenty-four countries and on every continent. It is possible that this record exceeds that of any other human.

Often, when I see people working with horses, it seems clear to me why a horse might be confused. We humans are far from perfect at understanding the mind of a species whose behavioural patterns are so far removed from our own. I wish I could live another hundred years because I believe we will 'get it' much better as time progresses. I often watch horses migrate through a road map of understanding as I do my work. I feel as though many of them would like to come back to me a month or so after a training session and say, 'Now I know why you persistently asked me to do something that seemed scary to me at the time. I can handle it now.'

Horses are extremely similar worldwide. The similarities far out-weigh the differences, whether you measure by breed or geographical location; and people are similar in the same way that horses are. I firmly believe that my educational background qualifies me to make these observations: I am a trained behaviourist and have travelled the world studying people and horses. Given these similarities, it is not surprising that horses respond to my concepts even when people believe, as they often do, that there is a need for unique treatment because of local tradition that has been in place for generations. 'Do not repeat a lesson as soon as the horse can do the task,' the racing trainer might say. The Western trainer might suggest that you hobble the horse. It is my goal to help horses by getting the message across to people that their nature is incredibly uniform the world over and that each of them wants to be dealt with in the absence of violence, pain and demand.

In my courses and lectures, I ask my students to spend some time getting acquainted with world maps. I tell them that it is hard for anyone to understand where they are, the direction in which they are travelling and where they want to be, if they have no knowledge of the world in which we live. When horses come into my round pen, they immediately orientate themselves to the surroundings. Horses have an incredible sense of direction. This is why old-timers will tell you, 'If you are lost, just turn his head loose and he'll take you home.' It is not simply an old tale; the horse will take you home. In my opinion, we need to learn a great deal more about where we are in the scheme of our goals and aspirations.

'True North' is generally the direction that travellers learn to identify in the course of becoming more familiar with where they are and where they are going. The North Star is often referred to as the focal point to identify at the start of any trip. It is my hope that, taken collectively, my answers will bring the reader to a greater understanding of where 'True North' is. I mean this from a philosophical point of view as applied to equine psychology. True training, true solutions to the questions can be found instead of quick fixes achieved through force, pain or fear.

In the answers I set out in this book, you will find a general consistency in approach. The solutions I offer will constantly return to the nature of the horse and meeting *his* needs, rather than simply citing the needs of the human and setting out to make the horse conform to them. I would like the reader to eliminate the phrase 'make the horse' from their vocabulary. Many decades of working with these wonderful animals have shown me the value of bringing the horse to want to do what you are asking of him, not demanding it of him through force.

It should be noted that the 150 questions included here are from real people who looked me in the eye and asked those questions out of a sincere desire to do a better job with their horses. I selected them from tens of thousands of questions, many of which went over the same ground to some degree. In these 150, I have tried to minimize repetition and still bring you the essential solutions you seek.

Enjoy your journey with me. I will attempt to be your guide along this pathway towards answers to questions that have been on the minds of horsemen for centuries. Please accept my answers as my best attempt to be accurate today. I am still learning, along with every reader. It is my hope that I can maintain an open mind until my last day.

Throughout this book I will refer to Join-Up® and the Dually™ halter. These are respectively registered and trademarked, and I say this now so that we don't need to add these marks after each reference from here on.

At the end of some of the answers I will add 'Recommended additional resources' and then one or more code numbers. These numbers correspond to items in the list of 'Recommended Additional Resources' at the back of the book, including further reading and other visual media.

ABOUT THE HUMAN

I have chosen to lead off with a few of the thousands of the questions that have come to me regarding us, humans, and how we think relative to our needs as horsepeople. This will help you to realize that working with horses is an act of reflection. I often tell people, 'When you can't figure out the problem your horse is having, the best thing to do is get a good night's sleep, get up in the morning and look in the mirror. What you see there is your horse's problem. You are required to get yourself right before you can expect to get your horse right.'

As you read the questions included in this book, try to answer them before you read my answers. It is an interesting exercise and one by which you'll find yourself steadily getting closer to the answers I have given. This is a form of imprinting whereby I consistently give answers based on the nature of the horse, and a student will gradually become more in tune with these concepts.

Question 1

I really want to become a horse whisperer. I love horses, and this is what I want to do for the rest of my life. I am twelve years old, but I know what my life's goal is. How am I going to get the information that I need to meet my goal?

Answer

I wish there was some way that I could explain in words how wonderful it is to receive this question. Questions similar to this come to me regularly. It is so gratifying to know that the world is changing and that young people want to become better educated in areas which allow them to work with their horses in the absence of violence.

You and others in your age group are the most important people in the world to me. You represent the future of the horse industry, and you give horsepeople a chance to apologize to the millions of horses that have been treated harshly over the centuries. Your question makes my life and all my work worthwhile.

It gives me great pleasure to be able to tell you that there are more educational opportunities for you today than there ever have been. I recommend that you read every question and every answer in this book. When you have finished, it is my hope that you will seek to take advantage of these educational opportunities. If you want to be a violence-free trainer of horses, it is critical that the first thing you do is learn their language. Once one has mastered the language *Equus*, then everything else becomes easier and more fun.

Having read the questions and answers, take a look at the 'Recommended Additional Resources' section at the back of this book. If you are dedicated to your goal, you will become familiar with all the material listed here. Having accomplished this, then you could look into the areas of formal education available to you. Learning the intricacies will take far longer; it is a lifelong journey to be the best you can, but certainly anyone, including you, can become a horse whisperer. Your stated goal makes you very important to me, as I have dedicated to my life to educating others in my concepts.

Recommended additional resources: 1, 15

Question 2

When I am witnessing an experienced horseman beating (I mean really beating) a horse in an attempt to get it to load, what do I do? Do I have the authority to intervene?

Answer

You have authority to intervene if the person is breaking the law. In this case, you should intervene. You can call your local emergency line and make a report – or the animal welfare hotline, if your community has one. If it's possible to videotape, you should do that so that the authorities can have evidence of the brutality.

One should not be silent in these cases. It is your duty to speak out. I am sure that you care for horses a great deal or you wouldn't have bothered to ask this question. Let's assume for a moment that it was a dog or a child being beaten. My recommendation would be the same.

It is not a good idea to confront violent people, especially while they are in a state of anger. It is not likely that one can make a significant difference while the brutality is in progress. It is, however, quite possible to make a great deal of difference by calling in the proper authorities.

Following these procedures can often prove to be a great favour to the violent person. He or she probably needs help and, if everybody simply turns his or her head away, nothing will change. Many of these people were trained to do their work using extremely harsh methods. They actually think they are right.

My goal as I work with people around the world is not to cast great blame on them, but to give them alternative ways of behaving. Not only do I tell them about methods I feel are more humane and effective, but also I demonstrate for them using remedial horses so that I can show by example. Maybe some day you can carry on my work.

Recommended additional resource: 2

Question 3

When I attend a competition, my jumper is OK so long as she is with other horses. However, when she comes to the point when we have to perform, she will be fearful immediately and does not trust herself to jump. A horse stressed by a competition, exaggerated by my tension, sounds logical to me. But I have never experienced such a reaction from other horses. I cannot punish her for this behaviour because it would make her more fearful. Would it be possible that her being separated from the other horses causes this behaviour? At home she does not like to be alone, but she normally gets used to it and becomes quieter.

Answer

It may be that separation anxiety is exacerbating this problem. If it is performance anxiety, it seems to me that you have a very clever horse. In fact, it almost seems as though she can read the newspaper, or the horse magazine that lists the upcoming horse events! Obviously, you know that this is not true, so let's investigate how this phenomenon occurs.

'Stage fright' is reserved for human beings with performance anxiety. It is not within the makeup of a horse to view any special occasion as more important than another and perform badly. The neocortex, the part of the brain that controls logical emotions such as planning, thinking and imagining, makes up only half the proportion of the horse's brain that it does in the human brain. Horses simply do not have the mental capacity to be capable of experiencing these feelings of performance anxiety.

As we negotiate the calendar of events we plan for our horses and ourselves, we should be well aware of our own mental state working up to and experiencing performances away from home. Whether it is a trail ride or a high-level horse show, these are circumstances where we tend to get our own adrenaline up and our pulse rate becomes higher than normal.

The one thing that horses can do far better than any human being is read the psychological and physiological state of the individuals around them. Mother Nature has provided them with incredible skills to identify potentially dangerous predators in their environment.

Given these conditions, it becomes incumbent upon every horseperson to learn to control their own responses to the stress inherent in big shows, little shows, trail rides and even a visit from someone they admire. Our horses will respond to our body conditions far more quickly than we ever dreamed possible.

Whether it is for your horse or yourself, it is good to take trips to public events, primarily to expose you both to a strange environment at a time when you are not competing. This will enable you to experience the environment, both physical and psychological, with low adrenaline. It will help you learn to control yourself as well as give the horse a chance to explore new territories without being asked to perform at a high level.

It is interesting that you say you have had other horses that acted acceptably under these conditions while this horse does not. One should be ever mindful of the fact that horses are uniquely individual. We tend to think that people are unique while horses are not. It occurs to me that this horse is far more sensitive to your physiological condition than the other horses were. Continue to test these ideas and observe the results.

Recommended additional resource: 1

Question 4

I have read your books and seen several of your DVDs. You often use the terms 'proper breathing' and 'low adrenaline'. Please explain to me how one is to go about altering breathing techniques or controlling adrenaline levels. I have tried to work this out on my own, and I don't think I am being very successful. It would be helpful if I had some tips on how one goes about controlling these factors.

Answer

As I work with horses in front of a group of students or in a public demonstration, I often say that one should work hard to keep adrenaline down. I suggest that it is important to study how to maintain as low a pulse rate as you possibly can. A lot of this has to do with learning the language *Equus* and being comfortable in the presence of horses, even those that might exhibit challenging behaviour. I often go on to say that one of the physiological factors that horsemen or horsewomen need to address is the art of breathing.

Students will generally laugh at this statement and tell me that they already know how to breathe perfectly fine. With that I might ask the student to demonstrate for me the art of diaphragmatic breathing. They will generally frown and give me a quizzical expression. It is likely that they have not heard of diaphragmatic breathing and just as likely that they know very little about proper breathing.

It is understandable, I suppose, that a student would ask what this has to do with horsemanship. My response is that it has everything to do with horsemanship, and for centuries horsemen have been successful or unsuccessful depending on their breathing abilities, even though virtually none of them knew of the existence of anything called diaphragmatic breathing.

One of the key reasons why those who became successful with their horses did so was that they could relax in the presence of their horses and remain in a fairly relaxed state throughout a given training session. Horsemen acquired this skill by working with horses for hundreds of hours. Typically, if we do something often, it becomes familiar, and familiarity tends to produce relaxation; so all this hands-on experience caused them to perform their tasks in a relaxed state.

Mother Nature has created within the flight animal a tendency to mirror the state of animate objects near them. This is what I call synchronicity. Physiologically speaking, when our pulse rate is up, theirs will elevate as well. If my adrenaline is high, chances are my horse has elevated adrenaline also.

Many decades ago I recall competing on a horse named Fiddle d'Or. He was a fantastic athlete, and I knew that if I could perform my duties successfully he had a chance of becoming my first World Champion. I was well on my way to accomplishing my goal when a challenging circumstance threatened my chances of success.

Fiddle was being shown frequently, which is typical with a campaign for a World Championship. As he became more and more familiar with the routines of the show ring, he began to anticipate my cues. When he acted on this impulse I became tense, anticipating his anticipation. This resulted in a jerky, disconnected performance, whereas the highest score would come from a smooth, flowing performance. I remember it was August, and with the year-end finals coming up in November, I needed to keep Fiddle performing at optimum levels for at least eighty more days and about ten competitions in order to have a chance of a World Championship.

We were in Monterey, California, when Don Dodge, a horseman whom I relied upon for coaching, suggested that I wasn't breathing properly. I clearly remember thinking it was a joke, and I was inclined to dismiss his words until I could see that he was very serious about his advice. I asked him where he thought I might go to learn to breathe, and he said that I should visit with the drama or public speaking professors in my university.

When I explained to the head of the drama department what my problem was, he had a good laugh. It was clear that he could not imagine how breathing could have an effect on the behaviour of a horse. He agreed to help me, however, and when I described Mr Dodge's use of the words 'diaphragmatic breathing' he seemed to know exactly how to proceed with the process of instruction.

Mr Warren began by showing me illustrations, which clearly outlined the anatomy of the human body. He concentrated on the torso. He showed me where the lungs and heart were located and described for me a flat muscle called the diaphragm. This structure separates the lungs from the intestinal cavity. The human body can cause the diaphragm literally to arc upward, becoming dome-shaped like the lid on a cooking pot. This can happen, for instance, if we gasp when frightened. He further stated that our anatomy allows us to cause this same muscle to sag downward into the intestinal cavity. 'The dome,' he told me, 'tends to intrude upon the lungs, which can heighten anxiety. Conversely, the sagging diaphragm tends to relax the whole body.'

He explained that singers who lift the diaphragm, consciously expanding the upper chest, tend to shorten the vocal cords, which compromises the quality of their voice and lessens their vocal range. He went on to say that those who learn to drop the diaphragm down, breathing into the stomach area, accomplish quite the opposite with their voice. Actors want a rich voice and relaxation at the same time; thus proper breathing becomes extremely important to anyone aspiring to the Broadway stage, or just to proficiency as a public speaker. I have come to realize over the past five decades that good horsemen should be aware that proper breathing could easily spell the difference between success and failure with the horses we are endeavouring to train and/or compete on.

Fiddle d'Or was the World Champion in his event that year of 1961. In great part because of what I learned, he also won the World Championship the next year, 1962. I am certain that, had I not learned proper breathing, it would have been extremely difficult to get him through that second full season of intense competition. It is my opinion that his performances would have lacked the fluidity necessary to be world-class. I have also come to know in recent years that proper breathing is at least as important when working on the ground as it is from the saddle.

When helping people with their riding, I will often tell them to relax and, as they breathe, to try to push their belt buckle toward the saddle horn of a Western saddle or the pummel of an English one. It is a human tendency to pull the belt buckle inward, consciously elevating the upper chest, which most people feel makes a more attractive human form.

It took me about thirty days to bring this skill to a sufficient level to have a noticeable effect in my horses. Like so many other aspects of our learning, one should not expect to achieve perfection overnight. I suggest two to three practice sessions of correct breathing per day, each of at least half an hour, until you are satisfied that you have mastered this art. I can now use diaphragmatic breathing as the main physiological way of reducing my pulse rate by eight to ten beats per minute. I have experimentally managed a reduction of more than twenty beats per minute in conditions of danger and stress.

In conclusion, I would suggest to any student of horsemanship that they too study the art of proper breathing. These days I am sure the information is much more easily gathered than it was in 1961. I can state categorically that becoming familiar with these procedures will tend to improve your overall physical and psychological health, whether or not you work with horses.

Recommended additional resources: 1, 6

Question 5

How does someone introduce your methods to those people who would sing the praises of traditional methods, that horses need to be shown who is boss? These people would suggest that the whip is helpful and immediate punishment is an effective way to train.

Answer

I think that the key to answering this question is to say that I would like my horses to do the talking for me. I believe that if I hold true to my concepts, the horses will continue to learn and perform well. There is no forcing the traditional horseman to accept my concepts. Just as I work without forcing a horse to do anything, I will never demand that another equestrian use my techniques. I would much prefer to be a good role model, advocating a non-violent approach to training and experiencing cooperative horses in return for that effort.

We need to be clear what we mean by 'traditional' methods. There have been many horsemen over the centuries that have worked traditionally but have minimized pain and violence, and many others who have maximized those elements. Traditional horsemanship as I saw it while growing up was virtually all done with what I would term extreme violence. Consequently, when I use the term 'traditional', it refers to methods which include what I would consider brutal treatment.

It seems to me quite clear that there are a percentage of 'old school' horsemen who will choose to go on using harsh techniques throughout their days. So long as their methods are legal, then there is very little that anybody can do about them. We are at a peculiar spot in the evolution of horsemanship. There are areas on this earth where certain actions are illegal while they are accepted in other locations. It is still legal to rope a horse by his legs in most parts of the United States, but illegal in some areas. It is still considered acceptable to four-foot a horse in Mexico, but it will put you in jail in California. Four-footing is the act of roping the front feet while the horse is in full gallop. This causes the horse to fall head first into the ground. This procedure was deemed illegal in the state of California only within the past ten years. The world is changing faster than the generations are rolling by. This results in cultural variations from one geographical area to another.

While I support whipless racing in the United States, there are still certain racing communities that levy a fine on the jockey if he doesn't whip his mount. Scandinavia, however, has virtually banned the whip altogether. Germany has a soft, spongy 'nerf' whip for use on two-year-olds. Apparently horsemen in these countries have come to realize that giving the horse a positive experience in the early stages of its racing career is more effective than causing it pain.

If you want to have a fight with a traditional horseman, just go up to him when he is trying to load a difficult horse after a show. Tell him that he doesn't have to use harsh techniques like whips, sticks, brooms, twitches, etc. When you wake up with a black eye, you may realize that it wasn't very effective to confront a violent person in the act of brutality.

Some of my students have been known to offer assistance. Once in a while this works, but most of the time it will get them an earful of profanity and an invitation to leave the area at once. I suppose it will suit me well to just keep doing my demonstrations, thus showing people that the horses have the final say in all of this, and if they respond favourably it is likely that we will have a good chance of seeing significant change in the next generation of horsepeople.

Recommended additional resources: 1, 9

Question 6

What do you say to people who have gone down the wrong path and feel guilt, for example a horseperson who has been using harsh training methods?

Answer

I say, 'Tell them to take a bath.' *Everyone* makes mistakes. I have tried it both ways. Don't beat yourself up over it; it's counterproductive. Most people who use traditional harsh methods slide into it through peer influence. If it happens to you, walk away. All you need to do is make the choice, then stand up in front of the mirror and say, 'I throw it away.' If it happens to someone you know, regard it as a privilege that they have seen the light. If someone comes to you for advice, be understanding rather than accusatory. Remember that it takes a good deal of courage to acknowledge the use of violence. One should regard a request such as this as an expression of confidence in one's ability to counsel against the use of violence. I recommend that one takes this responsibility seriously and responds with compassion.

I regard it as an honour to assist those who wish to seek a better way. I fully realize that we cannot change the world overnight, but that the people we help are likely to become spokesmen for violence-free training.

Question 7

I am afraid of catching my horse in the field. What should I do?

Answer

If you are afraid to go and catch a horse in the field, then do not do it. A horse can sense fear and has the potential to get you into a lot of trouble. Learn how to move around a horse and work with an older, trained horse before you take any chances out in the field. Once you can move around a horse well and you know where he is going, you'll be more comfortable catching your horse.

One should actually never have to catch a horse. The horse should catch you; and when you can do that by learning the language and accomplishing the appropriate Join-Up, catching will be the least of your worries. It would not be wise for me to simply set out here instructions on how to catch a horse. The act of coming together with your horse in a pasture or field should be viewed only as the natural outcome of a proper understanding of your partnership.

It is rewarding to understand the horse's language and natural tendencies, which then can be used to bring horses into a cooperative partnership with a human. There is no way that we can simply learn certain segments of horsemanship. Each piece of understanding is a part of a mosaic of comprehension and we need to relate each one to all the others until we have complete comprehension.

Obviously there are layers of equine understanding, some more complicated than others, but it is not extremely difficult to become conversational with the nature of your horse; especially given that there are greater opportunities for learning today than there ever have been. Should you choose to accept the challenge to educate yourself in the language *Equus*, you will be greatly rewarded throughout your life in all your relationships with horses.

The act of joining up with your horse involves moving through a language of gestures that I believe has been in place for millions of years. Through this effort it is possible first to encourage the horse to go away, and then to accept his decision to return. Allow it to happen and achieve that moment in which the horse chooses to be with you rather than away from you. It will be an effective tool, and you'll have fun with it too.

Recommended additional resources: 1, 3

Question 8

How do you respond to being called 'controversial'?

Answer

Probably most often the first thing I do is smile. The reason for the smile is that I consider myself utterly non-controversial. It seems to me that if the practitioner of a particular discipline brings findings to the table and these findings are new, then they can be argued by two distinctly different means. One is academic and the other is practical. It seems very difficult to me to classify as controversial something that the founder has been actually demonstrating for decades.

I don't ask people to accept my concepts because I explain them in a certain way; nor do I request acceptance without extensive trial. I have now been demonstrating my findings to the public for more than twenty years. I suppose I could have asked the public to accept my principles over those twenty years with just five or ten horses as examples. The fact is, however, I have offered in open public forum demonstrations of my work with more than seven thousand horses. Those horses have embraced virtually every breed on earth and covered disciplines in the hundreds.

If you study history in general, it becomes clear that when new ideas emerge, virtually all are considered controversial by many until reasonably proven. The status quo is nearly an immovable object and, in fact, as an academic, I am totally in favour of that. New ideas should have to jump through all reasonable hoops lest we follow bad ideas down counterproductive paths. There are plenty of examples of the public having accepted unproven concepts only to be negatively affected. It seems wrong, however, if we test a new idea and find it effective over a substantial period of time, still to classify it as controversial.

Added to this mix is the fact that I am challenging an eight-thousand-year-old discipline that has changed very little in all that time. I am suggesting that many traditional ways of training horses were far less than optimal and, in fact, frankly brutal. I'm not suggesting all traditional horsemanship was extremely violent, but most of it was. I never say that I blame those forerunners for their work; I often state one must understand that it is the only way they knew. I consider my task in life not to be judgemental, but to offer an alternative to what has gone before me. No one on the face of the earth can truthfully say that I have tried to force him or her to work with their horses by my methods. That would go against the very core of my principles.

Another ingredient one must consider is that a few people who knew my father suggest that I have spoken of his physical abuse in a gratuitous fashion. Some will say they knew my father and that he was a nice man to them and incapable of brutality. Obviously, those people have not read his book, or choose to ignore his own words when he talks about tying the legs of horses or hitting them on top of the head. Most domestic violence is conducted without public knowledge. I work in this field extensively now, and find that to be the case in the majority of situations.

In conclusion, before anyone labels me controversial, I would ask him or her to accept one factor. I would simply request that I am observed with the realization that I don't just tell the public what I believe is right; I show my work over and over again. If there is a true difference of opinion, I have no problem with that; but it is hurtful when words like 'controversial' are laid at my feet while I am openly demonstrating my work that has irrefutably proven positive results.

Recommended additional resource: 4

Question 9

I've read that you are working with children using the same principles that you do with horses. How do you make the transition from horses to children?

Answer

There is practically no transition necessary. It is far closer to being the same than to being what academics would term a metaphor. With two doctorates in behavioural sciences and a body of work ongoing in schools and universities, I believe that I can speak clearly on this issue. This is not a horse question, nor is it a human question. It is a question about life and the behaviour of animate objects. As horsemen it is our obligation to train our minds to think with a strong degree of cohesion when answering questions regarding the behaviour of humans and/or horses.

Obviously you don't put children in a round pen and ask them to run circles, but, in fact, it's quite close to that. The key principles involved with children are philosophically aligned quite closely to those I use with young horses. First, eliminate all violence and force! Next, create contracts where positive actions always receive positive consequences and negative actions always receive negative consequences.

The use of this method puts the parent or adult out of the business of using harsh techniques to punish. A parent or horseperson can seek to enforce the agreed contracts with recourse to consequences that are negative, but not violent. This method will assist horseperson, parent or teacher to remain far less emotionally involved in discipline and more likely to maintain low adrenaline levels.

One simply sets up the contracts, which are designed so that there is always a positive and a negative for each of the behaviours involved.

Should the children or horses choose to be negative, the discipline is already agreed upon, and they automatically know the disciplinary measures that will result. Conversely, when the child or horse is positive, then the parent or adult must stand ready to perform the positive consequences contracted.

Recommended additional resources: 2, 4

Question 10

Mr Roberts, I guess my question is, 'Why you?' Why do you think you made these discoveries when humans had eight thousand years to understand horses and suddenly you reverse the methods that preceded you?

Answer

Well, I guess my answer would be, 'I don't know.' Imagine for a moment visiting a class of children learning to swim. Let's say they were taking their third lesson. You might notice one child who seemed to be swimming very well. Suppose you asked this youngster, 'Why is it you're swimming so well and the others don't seem to have caught on?' I suggest that this child would say, 'I don't know; it seems easy to me.' I am the worst person on earth to try to answer this question. I have often thought that someone must have understood these concepts long before me.

Still, this question has been posed to me thousands of times and so I have thought about it a great deal. I have studied others to see how they accumulate their information when compared to me. It is clear that I was born with certain skills of observation. Also, one should keep in mind circumstances in my early life that I have written about before. I had a very difficult childhood. My father believed in harsh treatment that by today's standard would have constituted felonious child abuse. I was motivated to find ways to eliminate violence from my life. Imprinted to violence, it was extremely difficult for me to erase it from my own makeup, but harsh treatment as a child drove me to place a high priority on creating a better life for the horses that were so good to me. Remember that I began showing horses in competition before the age of reason. I suppose it's possible to surmise that it is easier for me to think in the world of horses than the world of people. Now I am committed to a non-violent existence for my horses, my students and myself.

In addition to being driven and possessing skills of observation, I am colour-blind. It seems to me that this simplifies my life. Camouflage means nothing to me. The animal kingdom is loaded with ways individuals can be difficult to see in their wild environment. The mustangs were no exception. I was able to clearly define their presence and monitor their movements without difficulty. I sincerely believe that this made a great deal of difference in how I logged their behavioural patterns. While I have not sought a scientific explanation for this condition, I find that most colour-sighted people seem to be sensitive to colour patterns that are meant to confuse the viewer. It is apparently nature's effort to allow wild species an opportunity to increase their stealth characteristics. Whether it is the bodies of these animals or even their eggs, camouflage is often the difference between life and death for many prey animals. I find that with my colour-blind condition I simply see the shape of the object without being confused by the colour shades.

I suppose it is quite possible there were horsemen who grasped these principles of dealing with horses long before there were means to communicate them. Quite possibly, before the days of aeroplanes, telephones and videotapes, someone worked in similar ways in the wilderness without even realizing that there was a difference between this way and what was to become traditional.

One thing for certain is that no one chronicled these concepts as I have outlined them. It is true that the Greek Xenophon wrote about working with horses in a slightly similar fashion. His writings date to about 360 BC and probably more closely approximate my work than anything written since.

I find it amazing that in 1996, when I launched my first book, most horsemen said that I was dreaming when I suggested that there was a discernible language that I dubbed the language of *Equus*. About four years later, traditional horsemen began to write that I wasn't the first one to discover it, saying they knew of people who talked about the language long before my time. Now, in 2007, I often hear, 'Well, of course, there's a language. We've known it all along.' It seems that this is an often-travelled path for concepts considered new and original. This doesn't bother me so long as the horses ultimately benefit from the discoveries I've made.

Recommended additional resource: 4

Question 11

Why do some people faint when they see Join-Up for the first time?

Answer

This is an interesting phenomenon that I had very little knowledge of prior to the mid-1980s, when I began to do public demonstrations. I remember clearly the first time it happened. It was on Flag Is Up Farms. We called an ambulance, stopped the demonstration and declared a one-hour recess while they took the lady off for emergency-room analysis. There was a lunch after the demonstration, and the lady returned with her husband to give us a report on her condition.

She first told us that she was five months pregnant, which heightened our anxiety all the more. She then reported that the doctors had diagnosed her with hypo-oxygenation, which means that she had held her breath, starving her brain of oxygen until she slipped into an unconscious state.

When asked why she held her breath, she told us that she didn't realize she was doing it. She went on to tell us she had been abused as a child, saying that she felt she had transposed herself to the position of the horse. She said she believed she was thinking how wonderful it would have been to be treated the way the horse was, instead of how she actually had been treated.

Since this first fainting, there have been dozens more. We have had many other medical opinions, most of which have come from attending physicians, as we have never resorted to calling ambulances after the first occasion. These people are generally unconscious for less than a minute or two and often remember most of the circumstances surrounding the event.

How well I remember one night here at Flag Is Up Farms. I was doing a demonstration for Ford Motor Company UK as part of a conference for Ford executives and their spouses. Five ladies fainted in one demonstration. That stands as the record to this day. Each one fainted within the same one-minute period. It was directly related to a good Join-Up with a formerly abused horse.

After the demonstration, I had a conversation with each of the ladies. All had been physically abused at some time in the past. Each of them remembered pretty much everything leading up to their fainting. All of them returned to the round pen within five minutes or so and were comfortable watching the rest of the demonstration, while being attended by people on my staff.

Abused horses tend to bring out this phenomenon more than any other one factor. It is a fact that all but one of the fainters have been female. It is further true that about 90 per cent said they had been abused in their past. Further evidence would suggest that they became transfixed on the procedure they were watching, and simply forgot to breathe. Fortunately, we have never had an injury in the course of these episodes, and I hope it remains that way.

Recommended additional resources: 2, 3

Question 12

What was your proudest moment in the show ring?

Answer

Showing horses in competition was my entire life for about thirty years. Many victories come to mind when this question is asked. The National Championship in horsemastership would certainly be high on the list. I was required to ride Western pleasure style and perform reining, as well as show jumping and park seat English. These riding competitions were followed by three days of written examinations. It was a great feeling to accomplish the National Championship in 1950.

The number one accomplishment on this list, however, would be the fourth World Championship, won riding Johnny Tivio. While I give him credit for his fantastic achievements, I felt great pride in being his human partner during those years when he sat at the top of the list of Western competition horses. I choose the fourth World Championship because I remember so vividly receiving the trophy saddle and blasting around the show ring celebrating his achievement. This championship came after most people had given up on his chances of winning for the fourth time. He showed us all that he was the very best.

As a student of horsemanship, one might ask, 'Where is the lesson in this for me?' I would answer by saying that the talent of Johnny Tivio was expressed so clearly that it literally taught me how to stay out of his way. Johnny Tivio, more than any other horse, certified the lessons of so many that went before him. He taught me to be reasonable with my requests and to seek out his needs and meet them. These are lessons that every horseperson can learn in order to improve their relationships with their horses, whether for competition or enjoyment.

Recommended additional resources: 1, 4, 6

Question 13

How can I find the patience to repeat training exercises again and again with the horses? And how do I recognize progress?

Answer

A strong belief in my concepts gives me the patience to repeat procedures again and again. I know that they will ultimately be successful and, once you come to that conclusion, it will be much easier for you to express the patience required in this effort.

The loss of patience, particularly in non-violent training, is counterproductive. I have had a lifetime to discover that losing one's patience will eventually be viewed as a mistake. It is my opinion that we should practise the art of observing our mistakes, allowing us to learn from them.

It is my strong recommendation to every horseperson that they learn the language *Equus*. Once we know the instinctual patterns of the horse's brain and the way horses communicate, we are far less likely to experience a loss of patience. The dictionary of the language *Equus* can be found in my textbook *From My Hands to Yours*.

A profound statement made to me in this context was, 'A good loser is a consistent one.' We must not be good losers. This does not mean that we fall on the ground pounding our fists, acting in an immature fashion. We must, however, feel the hurt of losing in order to be motivated to change our tactics. We should replay mental videos of the procedure in question. When we view ourselves losing patience, we should carefully note the outcome.

I have found over the decades that any time I lost my patience my re-run of the mental video would show that my horse and I took a step backwards. Horses are forgiving individuals and, if we are quick enough to rectify our mistakes, they will soon be back on a positive track. Recognizing progress is certainly an art form, but I have to assume that each of us has some idea of what we want from our horses and thus can recognize the positive track.

Learning the language and understanding the nature of the horse will fortify your confidence. These bits of knowledge will support your resolve to stay the course, watching closely for improvement that you can appropriately reward.

Recommended additional resource: 1

Question 14

Monty, you mention 'extrinsic' and 'intrinsic' quite often in your teaching. Please explain for us what is meant by these two words, and how they relate to training horses.

Answer

The definition of 'intrinsic' is: 'relating to the essential nature of a thing – inward'. 'Extrinsic' is defined as: 'not essential or inherent – originating from outside'.

In my courses at university, I vividly recall being tested on this subject. I received a very high mark for the paper I wrote. My professor was impressed with the choice I made to use horses to explain the theory of intrinsic learning versus extrinsic learning. He indicated to me that most of the students had cited human examples, but believed that my choice of a flight animal was more effective.

In my paper I stated that from a behaviourist point of view *there is no such thing as teaching, only learning.* I stated that knowledge needed to be voluntarily pulled into the brain by the student and that it was very difficult to push knowledge into an unwilling brain.

Teaching is an admirable profession. My point, however, was to show how much more important it was to produce intrinsic learning rather than extrinsic learning. Intrinsic is that form of learning that emanates from within the student, while extrinsic is something pushed at the student from an outside force.

Giving the horse freedom of choice, causing him to be happy when he achieves the goal, is intrinsic. Taking the whip to the horse, and then stopping the whipping when he does what you want, is extrinsic. It is my opinion that shouting, threatening and intimidating are also extrinsic in nature.

For instance, let's take the number one remedial problem on earth as far as horses are concerned. Every horseperson has experienced a time when it seemed impossible to get a horse to load on a trailer (horse box). Wherever I go on the face of this earth, I will find people agonizing over this issue.

More than 90 per cent of the horsemen of the world feel that they can pound a horse into submission. They are of the opinion that they can frighten the horse sufficiently so that he chooses the trailer rather than the whip. The fact is they do. It takes a good deal of time, however, and puts stress on the relationship the person has with the horse, usually leaving the horse in an unhappy state, making the next loading day even more difficult.

In demonstrations I show people that, using the horse's language, *Equus*, and an intrinsic approach – requesting instead of demanding that the horse enter the trailer – I can usually accomplish this procedure in a matter of a few minutes. After Join-Up and a session to help my horse to understand my Dually halter, I attempt to educate the horse to move in all four directions willingly. With these procedures in place, loading is normally quite easy. When the exercise is completed, the horse chooses to load himself and is in a contented frame of mind. He has learned from a positive experience. You can read more about the procedure of helping horses learn to load in a relaxed manner in the chapter on 'Loading, Vehicles and Transportation' later in this book.

Recommended additional resources: 1, 5, 9

Question 15

What do you say is more important to horse training: trust or leadership?

Answer

I love this question because it sits at the heart of everything we need to understand before we can be successful in life or with our horses. Leadership is certainly a wonderful quality and, by its very definition, we will find it difficult to rise above mediocrity in the absence of it. Leadership plays an important role in succeeding in our chosen fields, in our relationships with others and, if we have children, as parents.

Many important people throughout the centuries would be considered successful because of their leadership qualities. Winston Churchill, Gandhi and John F. Kennedy each made his place on the world scene because the masses chose to follow his guidance. I think by now you would guess that I am going to say that leadership comes first and is more important than trust. Actually, the opposite is true.

No one can be a leader for their horse or dog until they first establish trust with that individual. As humans, we tend to lie and misinform, creating a type of false trust. It is, however, very hard to lie to a horse or a dog. They can see through us like no human being is able to. Consequently their inherent perception is far greater than that of any human. Perhaps it is because they are less confused by words, responding above all to actions.

Trust is the most important factor we can generate in our relationship with our horse if we are to be successful in causing him to want to be our partner. Should we choose to *break* him, we might enjoy the services of a created slave, but we will not get the performance of a willing partner.

Leadership comes next, after you have demonstrated to the horse with Join-Up that you understand his language, allowing him to adopt you as a leader. As herd animals, horses judge our ability to lead by what they feel is capacity to protect, strength and consistency of actions. Each herd member relies on the others in a non-contentious, symbiotic way.

If we choose to cause pain, it will reduce the potential for trust and will gain us not leadership, but domination. Should we choose to dominate, we will be viewed as a predator and not as a herd leader. This may bring about submission, but is not likely to create a meaningful relationship.

For centuries the act of training horses was viewed as a leadership role, directed at achieving submission. This allowed trainers to experience a certain level of cooperation with their horses, but seldom created a horse that was a happy and willing worker. Through my concepts I ask that the horseperson first establish trust and then execute leadership without violence, pain or coercion.

Recommended additional resources: 1, 2

Question 16

I own a riding school and have been a professional dressage rider for most of my life. In creating this school I found that I needed to broaden the base of my disciplines so I brought in a trainer for show jumping and one who gives lessons in Western horsemanship.

We care for about forty horses in our yard and train most of the individuals we attend to. Each owner sets up about two riding lessons per week. Each training session is around forty-five minutes to one hour, and lessons are one hour in length. I feel that we are tending to create horses that are less than happy with their daily routines. My dressage horses are working with what seems to be a resistance to their efforts.

Each of the three disciplines experience horses with ears slightly back and exhibiting slightly halting demeanour, acting as though they would rather not work on the given day. Can you help me in an effort to produce horses that tend to exhibit a more generous attitude? I would like to see our horses acting as though they liked their work rather than disliked it.

Answer

This is an extremely interesting question and one that goes directly to the heart of what I perceive to be the value of the Join-Up concepts. It is possible that you have heard me say, 'I want my horse to want to do his work because he wants to, not because he is forced to.' I am sure you realize that it would be far better if I could physically see the training techniques utilized in your operation. In the absence of that, however, allow me to speculate a bit as to what is happening here and recommend a potential solution.

I have read your question closely and paid particular attention to the time frames you have outlined. It seems to me that there is specific time allotted for training as well as for lessons and I realise that there is a necessity to hold to a reasonable schedule based on the needs of your business. But what I believe is happening here is something that takes place in too many training operations worldwide.

Let me say first of all, however, that the horses involved have no knowledge of the time requirements that are critical to you. In so many operations such as yours, trainers tend to go to work in sessions or lessons with a desire to get as much done as possible in the allotted time.

It is with this factor in place that there may be a tendency to minimise warm-up time and maximise the time for training horse and/or rider. This scenario is a perfect recipe for creating a less than generous worker. When we break down these elements and put them on paper, virtually every horseman can see it easily. It's when we get caught up in our daily routine that we tend to neglect these elements.

Let me do my best to recommend a middle ground, which will be reasonable to horse, rider and operation. The first suggestion is that you meet with the other trainers involved, discuss these issues and agree to a routine acceptable to everyone. In that meeting I propose that all individuals agree to give up some of their training time, allowing for more warm-up time. This pre-training session should be quiet, slow and without demand on the part of the rider.

Utilising these techniques I have found that the horses tend to take ten to fifteen minutes of quiet warm-up time before entering a mode of generosity. If demands are placed upon them to execute athletic manoeuvres prior to their relaxed warm-up, they will tend to resent their work. It should be noted that during the course of a lesson this time can be used to work on rider position, at the same time outlining to the student what the day's efforts will consist of.

It has been apparent to me that the students themselves appreciate this routine and they too benefit from a gradual introduction to the day's efforts. Granted, you will probably accomplish fewer minutes of hardcore training but it is my opinion that the daily accomplishments will actually increase. I believe that you will find your horse is travelling with a happy ear and overall body language, which will lead to overall increased performance.

It is obvious that some horses take more time than others to indicate that they are ready to go to work. The observant trainer should be watching for a settled movement. I like to call it 'looking through the bridle'. Prior to achieving this attitude one will see horses adjusting their head position, moving left or right in their direction of travel and even tending to change legs periodically.

These manifestations seem to me to be a clear indication that the body is warming up to the daily requirements; efforts to produce athletic movements prior to the completion of this warm-up are very apt to produce a resentful attitude.

THE LANGUAGE OF *EQUUS*

Since this section deals with the horse's language, let me say that I don't believe there is any way to get trust until you know something about the communication system of the horse. People have been remarkably inquisitive about this thing called the language of *Equus*. So they should be; it's new to us. In a few decades, I predict it will be well accepted.

In 1948 I began a journey of learning that has consumed my existence for six decades now. The starting point of this journey was my discovery that horses had a language and that we could involve ourselves by learning this unique communication system. I can remember so well the moments of enlightenment.

The fact that *Equus* is essentially a silent language would qualify as my first major surprise in a long list of discoveries connected with the language of the horse. Realizing that I could emulate gestures understood by the horse was the second and probably most important epiphany I experienced.

The joy of being able to enter the world of the horse, to become a part of its existence through understanding its language has been indescribably gratifying. Thousands of people who have come to know this language have described the learning process as a life-changing experience.

Sceptics have certainly expended great effort on attempts to dismiss these discoveries with every sort of suggestion that no language exists at all. The fact is, however, that more than seven thousand horses have held true to the tenets I describe in front of millions of live witnesses in demonstration format. I have identified nearly two hundred separate gestures. Each of them has been tested thousands of times. Horses, deer, dogs, cats, some birds, fish and certainly human beings have all laid testimony to the effective character of these gestures.

It is a point of critical importance that this language can be taught to others. Were this not so, it would do little good for anyone to know about it. At this juncture, more than ten thousand students have taken advantage of the educational opportunities available, and over twenty-two instructors are now in place at locations across the world. It is quite possible that the understanding of the language *Equus* has now reached 'critical mass' and will continue in perpetuity.

Question 17

I purchased your book last week and am pleased that I have already learned some of your good horse sense through trial and error myself. A very inspiring read for a horse lover. I grew up a farm kid in a beautiful part of Saskatchewan. There was, and still is, lots of unspoiled room to ride, and I had the good fortune to have a horse while growing up. However, there is a lot of wisdom for me to gain yet. I have always wondered about an animal's language as well. I knew there was one, but I couldn't translate much of it. Is there more?

Answer

It is a long process for me to prove to myself and to be satisfied that my definition of a gesture is true and demonstrable. I am not fully satisfied that I have any further gesture identification to add to what is included in my books to date.

I applaud you for continuing to investigate the potential to identify further gestures and their appropriate meaning. It is my hope that one day I might be able to witness your work and assess your findings. Please continue to explore. It is fun, and who knows what you might discover.

It would not be right to leave you with the notion that the language *Equus* has been fully identified. I am certain that the future holds many discoveries in this area. I firmly believe that what we now know is far less than what is waiting to be discovered.

Recommended additional resource: 1

Question 18

How do you really know what the gestures you have identified actually mean?

Answer

This is a very legitimate question, and I believe that you will be slightly surprised by the answer. The definitions I offer are translations or interpretations, and I consider *Equus* my second language. Are my translations absolutely correct? I have no idea!

I know that I came to my conclusions after about eight years of working primarily with mustang horses, and then backed it up with approximately fifty-five years of experience. My interpretation of the horses' gestures is based on a trial and error system because I knew of no other way to decipher the meaning.

I am constantly advised by well-meaning people around the world that they have slightly different interpretations for various gestures. I keep an open mind, and I investigate these possibilities with the horses themselves. The interpretations that I have written about are my best efforts. They will remain in place until someone shows me there is a more logical translation for a particular gesture. Remember that I often say: 'I want no other student to be as good as I am; I want every student to be much better.' With that in mind, I encourage continued investigation of what horses mean by their gestures.

There are three European universities currently studying my body of work. They are attempting to qualify my findings through tests designed with academic expertise far more advanced than any I possess. This does not bother me, for several reasons. I want the horses to be understood, and so I want the truth; and I have confidence – a confidence based on all the decades of good relationships that have assisted me in understanding the equine mind – that my findings will be discovered to be at least very close to accurate.

I have written before that my early findings, in the late 1940s and early 1950s have stood the test of time. Refining my understanding of eye movement took a good deal longer than those early discoveries. The key discovery was actually made while working with deer. I've related the story of an old doe that took great issue with certain eye movements I made. Deer, you should know, have a flight mechanism about a hundred times more sensitive than that of horses. This makes them very strict teachers that charge you a huge price for a mistake.

Grandma, the old doe that became my teacher, spent months teaching me that snapping my eyes from one spot to another was a big mistake when dealing with flight animals. Dragging one's eyes in smooth transition will allow one to communicate far more effectively in the world of the flight animal. I tested what Grandma taught me with horses I was working with and found these discoveries to be valid. This was as recent as the late 1970s and early 1980s.

I constantly watch for opportunities to learn more about the language *Equus*, and I encourage you to do the same. Whether you make great discoveries or not, you will have fun with it, and also improve your relationships with your horses.

Recommended additional resource: 1

Question 19

Would you normally talk to a horse?

Answer

Sure. I might say, 'Hey, Shy Boy. How you doin' today?' Of course, I talk to him. But does he listen to me? Naw, probably not. What I mean is, he hears my voice, but he has no idea what I am saying. You cannot go out there and tell a horse to accept his first saddle, bridle and rider using words. Their language, *Equus*, is silent. It's a language of gestures. I cannot emphasize this strongly enough. I've started eight to ten horses in a day without saying a word. Should you choose, training your horse to respond to voice commands is fine. Most equestrians effectively use voice commands. You should be aware, however, that this is a habituated response. Until trained to voice commands, horses rarely respond to any of our sounds.

Question 20

What do you do with a horse that will only allow one person to ride it?

Answer

I find a horse that tends to trust only one person generally has a good reason. Most often, it is because that one person has treated him in an acceptable manner, while others have not. I do not accept the premise to the question, however, because I believe I could deal with the horse, instruct the rider and successfully enable anyone appropriate to ride him.

While it is understandable that you might believe that a particular horse can be ridden by one person only, I would like very much to bring you to realize that it is not a valid conclusion, and only an assumption on your part.

The instant someone comes along who understands the language *Equus*, and works with the horse for a few minutes to gain his trust, the horse will accept that other person into his life. Horses that exhibit this type of behaviour are looking for a friend even more than horses that have several human beings acceptable to them.

Once a solid understanding of the language *Equus* has been achieved, the theme of this question simply flies out the window. I know it is difficult to accept that, when the horse acts like Hannibal Lecter towards any person but one, but if one were to learn the language and act upon these concepts, my predictions would soon be in evidence.

Question 21

I often speak to my horse and ask her to turn left/right or stop or gallop, etc. and she successfully does what I ask. Do you suggest I should continue to do this or shall I return to the normal/traditional way of training?

Answer

Horses trained with voice commands are often quite successful in developing a learned vocabulary. It is my opinion that they never know what the words actually mean, habituating their response only after repeated requests of a traditional nature prior to responding to the voice.

Let's say you were from Hungary. You would probably speak Hungarian to your horses, which would mean that I would need to learn that language before your horses would respond to me. However, if you were to learn the language *Equus*, you could communicate with any horse in the world, regardless of which country they were born in. *Equus* is the natural language of the horse, born out of centuries of surviving as an animal that was food for the predators.

I do not suggest that you stop using verbal aids. I say 'whoa' to my horse when I want him to stop and I 'cluck' to him when I ask him to go. These are very similar to the sounds that you are using, and I don't suggest that they are wrong. I do, however, recommend that we couple these with the legs, reins and/or the headgear in the training process.

THE PSYCHOLOGICAL NATURE OF HORSES

Any study of the behavioural patterns of a species must include a hard look at what has created the species in question. The history of the horse has, in fact, created the nature of the horse. It has been so much fun for me to learn how the inherent tendencies of *Equus* have emerged from the imprinted experiences of the millennia involved in creating this wonderful species.

Equus, being a prey species, has been moulded by predation. The scientific data available would strongly lead to the conclusion that a horse-like animal has been in existence for fifty million years. The size, shape and character of these individuals have clearly been affected by evolutionary development: the survival of the fittest. The horses we know are typically something like ten times the size of a human. This was not always the case. In the early days of the horse's development, predators were often much larger and horses were much smaller than they are today.

Horses would need to grow bigger and run faster if they were to survive. They would also learn how to avoid danger through flight. Horses would finally come to the conclusion that if they weren't familiar with a certain object, they should take the position that it would kill them. With groups of horses facing death every day, the weaker individuals gave of their flesh quite early in life, leaving procreation to those that learned ways to avoid the menacing predators. In the earliest day of *Equus* there were very large flying predators. This fact led to the imprinting of a phobic fear of flying objects with the potential to swoop down on little horses. As horsemen and women, we have to deal with these inherent fears, which persist even in our modern-day horses.

It is critically important to learn the nature of the horse and about all the factors that went to make up their responses if we are to be knowledgeable partners in a trusting relationship with these four-legged friends.

Question 22

I have a horse that is very stubborn. When I try to lead him somewhere that he doesn't want to go, he just stops and nothing I can do will cause him to follow me. Sometimes I can get him to move with a carrot, but then he just stops again as we approach the spot where he refuses to go. Please help me.

Answer

This is a problem that I see all too often in the horse world and one which I normally can fix in a matter of a few minutes. It does, however, require a piece of equipment that I use constantly in my work. It is called a Dually halter. It gets small and less comfortable when the horse resists it, and larger and more comfortable when he cooperates with it.

22.1 When the horse resists the Dually halter, it shrinks, becoming less comfortable.

The Dually halter is made of nylon for strength and should not be used to turn a horse out in the field with. For the remedial problem you outline, one would attach a single lead to one of the training rings, and then use procedures as outlined on the DVD that comes with the Dually halter.

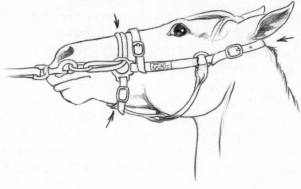

22.2 Arrows indicate where the halter shrinks and expands.

22.3 Arrows indicate the points of expansion, which add comfort.

This is one of the few problems that I can say with all certainty you can expect to solve in a very short period of time and with 100 per cent success.

Recommended additional resource: 5

22.4 The horse learns from the Dually halter that coming along creates comfort.

Question 23

Mr Roberts, you keep making a funny sound when you want your horse to go faster. You make a clicking sound with your mouth and sometimes you put your lips together and make a squeaking sound. Why do you believe that this makes the horse go faster?

Answer

To answer this question, I have to tell you the story of an incident that occurred during one of my classes at my academy in California. A lady asked this question, and I'm sure did so in good faith. It seemed a silly inquiry to me, and my answer was I did it because it works.

With that, the lady asked why those sounds make the horse go faster? My response was that it did and always has, so just do it. At the conclusion of the class session, one of my instructors came to me and reminded me that I had said many times that instructors should never tell students to do something just because they say it.

I was embarrassed by this reminder. I went to the student and apologized for my response and admitted to her I did not know why horses went faster when one made a clicking or squeaking sound. I told her they did and that it worked, but I simply didn't know why. I also stated I would attempt to discover the answer and get it for her and the rest of the world, if I could. I had never seen nor heard anyone ever address this before. It now became an obsession for me.

When I went to bed that night, I had little else on my mind. I am a visual person, and tend to re-run video-like images through my head. Often I will mentally train horses through the night, attempting to discover ways to improve the methods that I used during the previous day.

Watching documentaries on animals has been a favourite occupation of mine since childhood. On this particular night, I seemed to be re-running old films of African wildlife. I'm not sure whether I was asleep and dreaming or in a semi-conscious state, but I distinctly remember seeing a lion stalking a gazelle. I remember the lion carefully placing her feet on the ground as she closed in on her prey, stalking, low to the ground, as lions do. She would reach with a foot and then shake it a bit, seeming to clear the ground before she put any weight on it.

With this image, I jolted myself to a fully conscious state, jumped out of bed and circled the room explaining to Pat that I had discovered something no one else had ever reported. She humoured me by acting very interested in what I was saying as she fought off the interruption to her night's sleep.

Our class began at nine, and I could hardly wait to greet my instructor, my student and the class. I had about ten dry branches on the front desk when the session started. I went through the whole scenario of my discovery, and everyone had the chance to break a stick or two so they could realize how much it sounded like the clicking and squeaking that had started this whole inquiry. Once you realize that, it's easy to understand that the flight animal intends to put on a burst of speed whenever it hears what sounds like a stick breaking under the predator's foot.

My fifth book, *The Horses in My Life*, was a work in progress at that moment and thus it was here that I first publicly recorded this discovery. I invite the reader to find some dead branches and try this exercise. I believe you will see that the sounds are extremely similar.

Recommended additional resource: 6

Question 24

What do you do with a mare that pins her ears back when you feed her?

Answer

This is a phenomenon that is best described as 'territorial'. Horses, like many other species, tend to protect their food. It is a response of survival. Horses that become aggressive in the stable at feeding time should never be fed this way. Instead, one should take the horse away from the stable, put the feed in the stall and then return the horse to his or her box stall or corral with the feed already in place. Once the horse is in the stable and eating, one should respect the animal by leaving it alone.

If you follow this recommendation for a sustained period of time, it is likely that this undesirable behaviour will subside. If you continue bringing the feed to the animal's quarters, this aggressive behaviour could escalate to a level that is extremely dangerous.

Also, be sure to use the piece of good horsemanship, which requires us, when taking a horse into its box, always to turn the horse's head toward the door and release the horse only when one is at the door and the horse is fully in the loose box.

Question 25

Watching our horses as a group is an interesting bit of sociology. In particular, I am struck how the former boss of the herd (an old mare by the name of Kitten) during my teenage years is no longer the boss. A younger, working horse, Deuce, is now clearly the head honcho. How does this transformation take place?

Answer

Most of my life has been devoted to a great interest in behaviour and the social order of the family groups of flight animals. Obviously horses have been my main focus. I remember so well how surprised I was to find that the stallion was not the primary decision-maker within wild horse families. I like to tell my students that it isn't so much different from people. We men tend to think that we run the show when, in fact, a smaller, physically weaker woman really does. And I think it's quite valid that the important decisions made for the human family often rest on the shoulders of the mother.

I wrote in my first book about my experiences with wild deer. I explained how my first relationship with a deer was with one I call Grandma. She was a textbook matriarch, spending about ten months out of the year helping to raise the fawns of other does and keeping social order within the family group. This toothless old doe was still making the important decisions for the safety of this small herd well past the time when she had any offspring of her own. Grandma died of natural causes while still holding the position of 'matriarchal leader'.

Where horses are concerned, my experiences have shown me that the lead mare certainly shoulders the bulk of the duties regarding social order. It seems to me that, very much like the deer family, the equine family shows the matriarch a great deal of respect that seems to last well into the autumn of the life of the alpha mare. Unlike the deer, however, I believe that the horse family tends to read the female leader and, when she is no longer physically capable of staying up with the herd and assisting in its health and safety, will allow a younger mare to take over the position.

Typically this is a peaceful exchange of power and often it is passed from mother to daughter, if circumstances allow for that transition. This is one of the areas that I feel needs to be addressed where mustang capture is concerned, as this is often done in a manner that disrupts the smooth flow of social order. The transition of male leadership is, in my opinion, less important than the exchange of female leadership, but certainly that is an important factor as well.

It is commendable that you have made your observations, and I thank you for being interested enough to ask the question. You are in a position to continue your observations and draw conclusions about the individuals in your group. If more horsepeople chose to understand the social needs of our equine partners, it is likely that we would come to understand them better and develop a more compassionate approach to the relationship we have with them.

Recommended additional resource: 1

Question 26

In your opinion, Monty, do animals grieve?

Answer

It is my opinion that horses can grieve. I further believe that for the most part grieving takes place when the animals can see the dead or dying. Once they are apart, grieving normally stops very quickly. Many animals grieve for days after the loss of an offspring, and I believe horses fall into this category.

It has been said by American Indians I have known that they watched mares dragging a dead foal using their mouths at the crest of the foal's neck. I have been told that some mares would take the foal with them for about three days before giving up.

We know that dogs grieve and literally bury dead puppies. In my animal behaviour studies, I have learned of a mother elephant carrying a dead offspring for well over a week before resigning herself to the death of the baby. It seems that each of the species involved resolves the situation relatively quickly when out of the sight of the dead body.

Question 27

I love my horse, and I think my horse loves me. He follows me around already. Do I still need to do Join-Up?

Answer

Join-Up is a condition that follows a logical line of communication. It is a piece of completed communication that informs the horse that you are aware of his or her language and that you understand it. It has far less to do with love than with understanding.

With few exceptions, I recommend Join-Up as a communication effort with every horse that I work with. It builds the foundation for a mutual understanding between horse and human, which in turn results in trust and the earning of that trust. I appreciate your position that the horse already accepts you, and I understand why you would ask whether Join-Up is still necessary. I would suggest that, when properly executed, it always helps and never has negative effects. The exceptions might be orphan foals or aggressive stallions. These constitute another subject and should be left to the professionals.

What I need to do to bring you to a greater understanding of these concepts is to explore for a moment the definition of Join-Up. It is not a simple acceptance of one another by horse and human. It is far more than a simple curiosity or even a strong bond. Join-Up, within my concepts, is a procedure, and something far greater than what you have described with your horse.

Join-Up is that moment in which the horse decides that it is better to be with me than to go away. This is achieved, however, only after a body of work that is designed to inform the horse that you understand his language and you are prepared to live by the principles inherent in him after millions of years during which his nature has been imprinted with certain rules.

Join-Up and the understanding of the language of *Equus* are used to convince the horse, through a series of carefully designed exercises, that you mean no harm. Violence can play no part in this process. The horseperson must live up to the trust he or she engenders. We must agree to adhere to the tenets of non-violence or not use these principles at all.

Recommended additional resources: 1, 3

Question 28

What is the most important factor in causing a horse to accept his lessons?

Answer

If I were required to give a one-word answer to this question it would be 'trust'. There is virtually no way forward in education in the absence of trust, whether you're dealing with horses or humans. My students often hear me say 'adrenaline up, learning down', but how do you get adrenaline up, other than through fear and lack of trust?

It's a fact that trust is just the catchall word to describe contentment, relaxation and the desire to work in a partnership. Fear will only create performance for a short period of time before resentment and discontent strip the student of the desire to perform.

In reading your question, I am focusing on the phrase 'accept his lessons'. There are two distinct ways in which a horseperson can cause a horse to accept his lessons. One is through trust, and the other is through fear. The latter has been used for eight thousand years. The word used to describe the training process in most languages is 'break'. This word describes quite well the act of forcing a horse to do something or suffer pain. The sentence I most often use to describe this training theory is, 'You do what I tell you to, or I'll hurt you.' It was considered effective and acceptable for all of those eight thousand years.

After the global impact of my first book, many people began to see the shortcomings of applying force to a flight animal. Through demonstrations, I was able to cause horses to accept their lessons freely. I have displayed these concepts in the presence of public audiences with over seven thousand horses. No horse has been a failure.

The world is changing, and it is happening more rapidly than I could have ever dreamed possible. Tens of thousands of horses are trained each year following my principles, and they are performing far better than when they experienced training with force, pain and violence. I have no idea why it took so long for the human species to understand these principles, but I am very pleased that we are finally coming to know them.

There are more ways to be educated in non-violent horsemanship today than ever before. Be inquisitive: seek out the best information available, read the books, watch the videos and work with the horses. Once you are on your way to learning these concepts, allow the horses to be your teachers. They will always have the answers we seek if we will just be respectful and observant.

Recommended additional resources: 1, 3, 4, 9, 13, 14

Question 29

I have an almost eleven-year-old Spotted Saddle Horse/Tennessee Walker gelding. He had been a breeding stallion. He is a slightly high-strung horse, yet at home he is the sweetest, mischievous, most curious sort of guy. I enjoy showing him, but travelling makes him extremely stressed. I am now going to try some herbs as well as some Rescue Remedy. Other than that, do you have any suggestions?

Answer

If your horse was a breeding stallion, and has now been castrated and is still displaying the behaviour of an entire male then he must be treated as an entire male. I feel very strongly that no professional horseperson should advise anyone to use a stallion for pleasure activities; this includes horses that manifest the characteristics of an entire stallion. It is my opinion that this horse is acting on natural craving when he is transported to a horse-filled environment that is unknown to him. I am a believer in Rescue Remedy and other homeopathies, but I do not believe that they can guarantee you will overcome the problem you are having. It is not advisable to continue to transport this horse to showing environments.

While it's true that I showed stallions in competition for much of my career, I never felt that I placed myself or other contestants in harm's way. We must be responsible towards our horses, other contestants, the general public and ourselves as well. If I am writing this answer for a bona fide professional who is accustomed to handling stallions every day, it certainly takes on a different perspective from the answer I would write to a horse lover who competes periodically.

Many organizations operate with regulations against stallions in competition, and that addresses the issue in a few instances. Many horse-show associations have no regulations against competition on a stallion. It is my opinion that a great deal more attention should be paid by these governing bodies to the safety of the individuals involved. As a qualified judge of the American Horse Show Association, I consider all inappropriate male behaviour to be the same whether it was exhibited by a gelding or a stallion.

Once a stallion has entered a breeding mode, it is very difficult to cause him to realize when it is appropriate for him to express himself in this area and when it is not. We cannot expect a stallion to understand that a particular occasion is a horse show and not an opportunity to mate. This is beyond their inherent capabilities. Once the course of breeding has been initiated, it is advisable to confine their activities to those that are safe within these conditions.

Recommended additional resource: 1

Question 30

How much time do you have after your horse has made a mistake to correct it effectively?

Answer

Most of the leading behaviourists of the world will agree that where horses are concerned we have about three seconds after the action in which to reward or discipline effectively. One should remember that humans are much more apt to discipline immediately than we are apt to reward immediately. Since reward is every bit as important as discipline, we will tend to fall far short in that category.

In my world of training, the disciplines and rewards are quite simple. The creation of work will serve to discipline and the cessation of work shall serve as reward. While these are the main tenets, we can certainly vary their application. Work can be cantering in small circles or trotting up a steep hill. In addition to stopping work, one can dismount and create a rest session as a major reward.

There are many variations in the reward and discipline scenario. If you accept the basis tenets I have outlined, and build on them imaginatively, you can create appropriate solutions for each particular horse, taking into consideration its breed, discipline and temperament. Clearly, I suggest no violence or even elevated adrenaline in these efforts.

Psychiatrists and psychologists have a rule that governs this phenomenon, often labelled PIC/NIC, where PIC stands for Positive Instant Consequences and NIC stands for Negative Instant Consequences. The key word is 'instant', recognizing that we have three seconds in which to express contentment or discontent with the actions involved.

If your horse seems to be a slow learner or continues to cause you trouble, I suggest that you look inward to find the problem. Every horseperson should understand that horses are reactive. They will respond to our actions, creating very few on their own. If we are to discover the root of our horses' troubles over a sustained period of time we must scrutinize our own actions and this includes taking a hard look at the timing of the PICs and NICs. Bad behaviour is almost always our fault and not the fault of the horse.

Recommended additional resource: 1

Question 31

How do you reward a horse that does not like to be touched?

Answer

In the Join-Up process a major reward is to walk away from the horse. Since this does not require touch, it is easy to do. Walking away, however, should be used only when the horse gives you positive responses. No mustang I have ever worked with allowed touching at first. However, over the years all mustangs that I have worked with found value in it eventually.

It is the obligation of the human to find a place on the horse that is possible to touch. Often it is high on the shoulder near the withers. This is a magical spot on the equine anatomy. It is where bonded horses scratch one another in the herd as a gesture of friendship. Their mothers from birth scratch baby foals in this area. This imprints them to allow touching in that area so long as they trust the one who touches.

Obviously, it is not good enough to stop the process after you can touch this area. If one learns *Equus* and acts appropriately in the horse's language, one can build upon this zone of acceptance quite rapidly, always remembering to walk away after each touch. Under normal circumstances I will be touching the forehead of any horse within a few minutes.

After causing the horse to allow touching and stroking, separated by periods of walking away, I then normally begin to work with a stick to scratch my horse in various areas, and very shortly the stick will have a plastic bag on it or a piece of cloth. All of this begins the process of not only allowing touching, but also establishing a level of trust sufficient for stroking and even putting equipment on. It is important to stay safe at all times. If necessary, one can work with an artificial arm first to reduce the risk of getting kicked. This procedure is described in the chapter of this book entitled 'Wild and Dangerous'.

In order fully to understand the process of causing a horse to trust you enough to let you touch it, it is absolutely essential to learn the language *Equus*. One should remember that there are more ways to learn these non-violent methods today than there ever have been before. It is fun to work with these concepts, and I am sure that horsepeople who take the time to educate themselves will find them more effective also.

Recommended additional resources: 1, 13

Question 32

Is it harder to get a very dominant horse to do Join-Up than one that seems to be normal?

Answer

Yes, it is a bit harder, but when I say a bit harder, I mean just that. While it may be slightly more difficult, I recommend that you do not dwell on the negative. The toughest Join-Up is so much easier than the best of the traditional methods that one should look forward to having fun with the process. Do Join-Up, and count your blessings.

It is a fact that I do Join-Up with more than three hundred horses per year all over the world. I believe it is fair to say that some of my best Join-Ups are accomplished with horses that are considered dominant. I think it's also true that some of my best Join-Ups are completed with horses that are considered shy and submissive.

The fact is that many of the best Join-Ups are accomplished with horses that are outside the mainstream of psychological normality. These are the horses that are seeking security and friendship even more than those that sit in the middle of the psychological spectrum. This is the same phenomenon that keeps me coming back to work with youths at risk. Young people who need you most will ultimately make the greatest change when you get your work right.

Recommended additional resources: 1, 13

Question 33

I had two horses at home, and I brought in a new one. One horse accepted him and the other did not. Can you help with this?

Answer

It is important to introduce a new horse gradually. Horses have a social pecking order. Failing to address this issue can result in injuries to your horses.

First you need to create a situation where the horses can communicate over a safe fence. The process is often called 'buddying up'. Only when you can sense complete comfort between the old and the new horse should you attempt to place them both in the field together. This can take two or three days, or possibly up to two or three weeks.

Many people will tell me that they don't have an area with a safe fence for the horses to communicate over. They will often add that they just don't have the funds to build a fence. In these cases I suggest other ways of bringing about the same situation. One would be a box stall with the resident horse outside and the new horse inside and able to put his head over the door.

If that scenario is not available, another possibility is the use of a particular kind of electric fence. This involves a strip of tape, usually about 2 inches wide, with metallic strands running through it carrying a low current. One does not want to shock any horse. This is especially made for horses, and it produces a tiny tingle. Horses are extremely sensitive to this sensation, and they will respect its presence very quickly.

When your horses become accustomed to it, it is a very effective way of keeping them separate, but allowing them the sight and smell of one another and even some nose rubbing. I have seen horses scratching one another on the withers over this tape and never touching it.

The bonding process is quite fast, and if you observe your horses, you will find them migrating towards one another before you risk putting them in together.

Once the new horse is in the field with the other horse, then if you have bullying, you simply turn the tables on the bully. When he acts out against the new horse, immediately stick him behind the tape in a small corner of the field. Leave him there until you notice a more reasonable acceptance of the new horse or a desire to get together with him again, and then test his intentions. Should he act out negatively, repeat the process.

Recommended additional resource: 1

Question 34

Does yawning have a meaning for horses?

Answer

It certainly does, and it has a critical meaning when training horses. The point of yawning is to take in oxygen. One element of tiring is starving the brain of oxygen. During exertion and tension we assign oxygen to muscles needed for work. Horses in their quest for survival will enter periods of extreme physical stress when they steal oxygen from the brain. They'll push themselves for a long time, and then, when they become satisfied that they are not going to die, they'll relax and yawn because their system is taking over to re-oxygenate the brain.

When I work with horses at starting gates on the racetracks of the world, I sometimes find that it can take up to a couple of hours to achieve this state. It is a demonstrative act that means, 'I'm relaxed now, and I feel assured that you're not going to hurt me.' In my early days of remedial work with horses in the racing industry, I remember thinking that it was just a coincidence. As my experience bank increased, it became clear to me that it is a normal physiological response.

Stealing oxygen from the brain does not occur because of all-out exhaustion; it occurs because the concerns within the flight animal set the wheels in motion to prioritize the supply of oxygen to the areas that will enable them to run for their lives. Once that requirement seems to have been satisfied, then they will begin the process of re-oxygenating the brain.

Horsepeople should not feel that this is either a good or a bad thing. It is simply the nature of the animal we are dealing with. If we are to train in the absence of violence, pain and pressure, then we must address the needs of the horse within its own physiological and psychological parameters.

Question 35

Monty, what do you think? Do horses dream?

Answer

'Do horses dream?' is a question that has been bandied about for generations. Every dog owner is certain that dogs dream, so why not horses, too?

I was in Monterey, California, in 1958 at a horse show and Pat entered us in a mixed team roping. Since I didn't own a decent rope horse at the time, Pat had borrowed two horses from her cousin. I asked what I was going to ride in the open roping and she replied, 'Old Sergeant!' Sergeant had been a darn good heel horse in his day and was about seventeen or eighteen at the time of this event. I liked Sergeant. It was a good choice.

The two roping horses were delivered to the fairgrounds. They had been used on the ranch and, while one had shoes on that were adequate, Sergeant's feet looked terrible. I asked Pat to make arrangements with the on-duty farrier to get some new shoes on him before the competition began the following day.

The farrier was Bill Whitney, an old friend who'd been our farrier for most of the post-war years on the Salinas Competition Grounds. Bill was quite old by this time, and he asked me if Sergeant was gentle. The horse had burrs in his mane and tail and his overall raunchy look suggested he might be a bit wild. I reassured Bill that I had roped on him dozens of times and there was no question that Sergeant was gentle. That was a given.

Bill suggested I should return in about an hour and a half. Pat and I called in at the horse show and rodeo office to go through the necessary check-in routine, had a hamburger and then moseyed back to collect Sergeant. As we walked up, we both realized that something was wrong. Bill's assistant was walking briskly to greet us and he had a disconcerting look about him. I guess his eyes were open just a little too wide and his shoulders seemed to be a bit stiff.

'Bill's gone to the doctor,' he said. 'Sergeant kicked him and they took him away in an ambulance.'

'What?' I replied. 'That's not possible. Sergeant's never kicked anybody in his life!'

The assistant told us that Sergeant had stood without incident while three shoes were easily fixed in place. In fact, he was so placid and calm it seemed like he'd fallen into a deep sleep while being shod. Then, when his leg was picked up for the last shoe, he suddenly exploded, blew hard through his nose, kicked out, pulled back and tried to run away all at the same time, and caught Bill on the leg. It was incomprehensible.

The assistant agreed to put on the last shoe, and while he was doing it Bill appeared. He had a slight limp and showed us that he was wearing a bandage under his jeans. We asked what he thought had happened. Fortunately, Bill had a big smile on his face.

'Monty, I disturbed that horse while he was dreaming about a lion,' he said. 'There's no doubt in my mind about it.'

Sergeant never made a move while the last shoe was nailed on, and Pat and I were able to rope. Bill Whitney was OK to continue his shoeing for the balance of the show.

I've had many dreams about horses – Pat has often been woken by an arm landing across her face when I dream of being bucked off. As a child, I often dreamed of riding into the mountains, hiding away, escaping. Then I would watch myself getting stuck in the wrong place – dreams of panic and pursuit. When I was dealing with Barlet (a mean stallion), I dreamed of being devoured by a horse.

But do horses dream? Who knows – I suppose the debate will continue until someone straps a machine on a horse that proves it one way or another. For me, I'd just like to continue thinking they do, but never knowing for sure.

Recommended additional resource: 6

Question 36

I am new to horses and my lovely mare Layla has produced her first foal, now nine weeks old. I haven't been able to find anything as to how you would start them off. So far I have been stroking her. I started with the top of the tail. Her little brush goes straight up in the air and her ears go into the relaxed position. Then I slowly travelled up her spine ending by scratching her withers. I have just begun stroking her flank while slowly going down her legs. She is a delightful little horse and backs up to me now for her bum scratch. Am I doing this right? How do I start her to a headcollar? What would you suggest? Your book is my bible.

Answer

One must be careful about playing games with foals. It may seem fun when they are tiny, and too small to do you much physical harm. But these little characters grow up very fast, and they take their habits right along with them. If you are not careful, you may create a yearling that will back up to you and, if it's not satisfied with the scratch it receives, just might kick you. Backing up to you is not a good habit to encourage.

My textbook includes extensive information on the rearing and early training of young horses. It is the only book that I have written which deals with the 'how to' and 'hands-on' elements of my concepts. In it, you will find that I recommend a Dually halter for the early training of horses. Further, you will discover that I use the particular piece of equipment called the 'foal handler'. There are many aspects to rearing a young horse properly, and these are covered in depth.

Foal imprinting is a procedure that I recommend. It is the introduction of the human in the first hour of the foal's life. It is my opinion that it helps the mare to accept her foal, and it certainly helps the foal to accept human beings. The use of a foal handler is very helpful. It is fashioned with a piece of rope in a figure-of-eight configuration. It circles the shoulders and hips of the foal and allows the handler to control the youngster without aggravating restraints.

Once the foal is weaned, the Dually halter will be extremely helpful in creating a willing animal with appropriate ground manners. It will assist you with the process of leading forward, stopping, backing up and respecting the space of the handler: all essential procedures in the early training of foals. When we get this work right, we build a foundation for a good relationship throughout the life of our equine friend.

Recommended additional resources: 1, 5

Question 37

Do you ever have a horse that does not respond to your methods?

Answer

No. However, I believe it is fair to say that they are not really my methods. They are concepts that I have observed in nature. It is probably better to say that they mirror the natural behaviour of the horses themselves and so, if they are properly executed, there is no way to fail. Should the horseperson experience negative results, it is important to look inward. It is undoubtedly not the fault of the horse.

Having outlined my beliefs on this subject, it should be said that I have only worked with sixty or seventy thousand horses in my lifetime, including a list of over seven thousand horses that I've worked with in front of public audiences. While these are large numbers, they are certainly not anything close to a majority of the horses on earth. Maybe I will have to answer this question differently after the next horse I work with.

Even if that next horse could be considered a failure, though, it would be because of something that I could have done differently and not the fault of the horse or the method. Horses' motives are pure; they mean no harm to anyone. They can't lie, nor do they contrive or conspire against any other individual, human or otherwise. If we can work with these tenets clearly in place, we can become better horsepeople. In fact, we will become better people, too.

Question 38

An old-timer told me that horses of different skin colour have different sensitivities and that the darker the skin (like true black), the more sensitive a horse will be. He told me that greys are the least sensitive and will take all kinds of kicking and/or spurring while a black horse will not tolerate it. He also said that sometimes the way a horse is being ridden, if it happens to have sensitive skin, would cause the horse to appear to be rank, nervous or unmanageable. For example, some horses might start bucking because a person is putting their heels into his or her side, which shouldn't normally be a problem except the horse is just extra sensitive. What is your experience with this? I have found that it is even true with dogs.

Answer

Without scientific proof of my theories, I will explain to you what experience has taught me over the past six decades. It seems evident to me that many people concern themselves with hair colour where sensitivity is concerned. I believe that it is far more important to look at the colour of the skin than the colour of the hair. If we accept these premises then the black horse with black skin sits on one end of the spectrum and the true albino sits on the other.

I don't believe that either of these assumptions is necessarily correct. I am also of the opinion that it is quite incorrect that black horses with black skin are the most sensitive; in fact, I believe that they tend to be the least sensitive. The best evidence that my assertions are correct comes from the companies that produce counter-irritants used to increase circulation in joints. Most of their labels will caution users to reduce the application for chestnuts and other horses of light skin colour. For the past eighty years or so, these companies have observed that chestnut horses with white legs that have light-coloured skin are far more sensitive to these substances. I have personally experienced significant oedema with white-legged chestnuts, even when preparations were administered at half dose.

It is my opinion that light-skinned horses have nerve ganglia closer to the surface and so tend to be more sensitive than dark-skinned horses. In the absence of scientific proof, let me relate to you circumstances that at least add weight to the theory that chestnut horses are more sensitive than the darker ones, and fillies more sensitive than their male counterparts.

It was 1985 when I did my first public demonstration. Between then and now, drawing on over two decades of such work, I have obviously logged many experiences regarding the nature of the horses that I work with. In 1990 I was on tour in England for Queen Elizabeth II. Her Majesty was most interested in my bringing my concepts to as many British horsepeople as I could.

The horses were brought to me from hither and yon. Each community would find a different group of untrained and remedial horses for me to deal with. I recall a demonstration evening in Blewbury, Oxfordshire. I mentioned to the lady who was in charge of dealing with horses and owners that it seemed to me about half of all horses in the UK were chestnut fillies.

Faith Gray was the lady's name, and she had a real laugh at my statement. Of course, she said, they save all the chestnut fillies for when you come. I inquired why that was, and she told me that everyone knew that chestnut fillies were the most difficult to handle. This is not something that had ever occurred to me prior to that time, and I had been dealing with horses for more than fifty years.

Since those early days, I have found this to be a general feeling right across the world. Horsemen will report that chestnut fillies are worse to handle for the farrier or the veterinarian, and certainly more sensitive to their first saddle and girth. There seems to be a general consensus that light-coloured chestnuts have a more sensitive nervous system than horses of any other colour, while most horsepeople feel that fillies are less tolerant of prolonged training sessions and tend to get crankier than colts or geldings. I would tend to agree with that theory.

Question 39

My horse won't change legs. What can I do?

Answer

In order to answer this question so that it is understandable to readers at all levels of horsemanship, it is necessary for me to describe what changing legs means and why it exists. I have described this in great detail in other written work, so I will attempt to be as brief as possible in this Q&A format.

39.1 This illustrates the initial foot fall at the canter, creating Beat 1.

Horses have four legs. At the walk, each leg strikes the ground individually, creating a four-beat gait. At the trot, the feet strike the ground in pairs, creating a two-beat gait. At the canter, one pair of legs strikes the ground individually while the other pair meets the surface at the same time, thus creating a three-beat gait.

In executing the three-beat gait, nature has provided that one side of the animal becomes the leader, thus sending that pair of legs a greater distance with each stride. Any given horse, when travelling in the third gait (canter/gallop/run) tends to lead on the side towards which they are making a turn or intend to make a turn.

This means that if a horse is cantering in a circle anti-clockwise, it is comfortable for him and considered correct if he is leading with the two left legs. Conversely, if he were cantering clockwise, it would be comfortable and proper to lead with the two right legs.

The question I must deal with has to do with changing the leading leg.

This can typically be accomplished in two distinctly different manners. One is a simple lead change, which is generally accom-

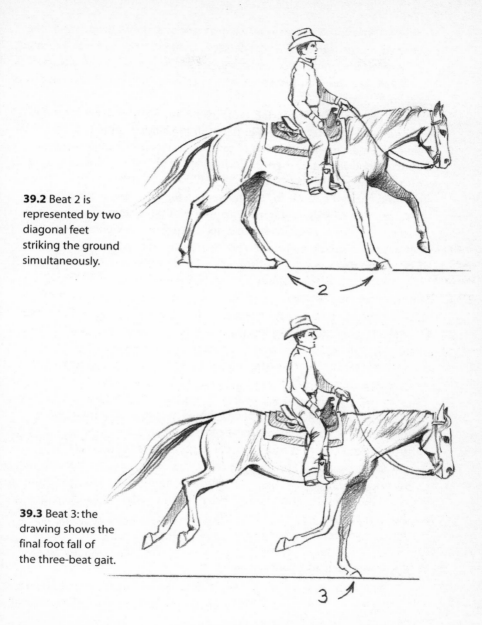

39.2 Beat 2 is represented by two diagonal feet striking the ground simultaneously.

39.3 Beat 3: the drawing shows the final foot fall of the three-beat gait.

plished by reining back to a two-beat trot and then advancing to the canter on the opposite lead. The second manner would be to execute the more complicated fly lead change. That becomes a more advanced manoeuvre and requires a good deal of training for both the horse and rider.

If the rider is comfortably cantering in a circle, large or small, bending slightly left and his horse is on the left leg, all is well. Should the rider decide that he wants to change directions and travel in a circle bending right, then the principles of flying leg changes come into play.

Leg changing, both for the horse and for the rider, is an art form. Nature provides the horse with an inherent talent to change leg. It is when a person is involved that leg-changing problems arise. The weight of a saddle and rider, and, more importantly, what the person does with that weight, are absolutely critical to the act of changing legs.

The one tip that I would like to bring to the reader in this Q&A format is that leg-changes are easiest for the horse to accomplish when the spine is relatively straight. The rider who tries to cause the horse to change leading leg by demanding that it change direction quickly is likely to have great difficulty. It is important to establish a relatively straight travelling direction prior to making the flying change.

In my show career, leg changing was one of my strongest suits. It is my opinion that the act of changing legs properly should be a free ticket: that is, there should never be a question about being on the proper leg, because it's just as easy to get it right as to get it wrong.

Obviously, any art form must be learned, and there is a specific set of procedures that are necessary for both the human and the equine student. If a reasonably talented rider becomes educated and executes the appropriate manoeuvres, it is highly likely that the horse will perform proper leg changes.

Recommended additional resource: 1

Question 40

How do you make a performance horse more valuable?

Answer

I am a firm advocate of never making a horse do anything. But this type of question is often asked of me. The only way that I know to elevate the value of a performance horse is to reach a higher level of excellence or win more competitions. The only way I know how to win more competitions is to reach a higher level of excellence. The only way I know to cause a horse to reach a higher level of excellence is to cause your horse to *want* to excel, not to try to force him to excel.

Nutrition and grooming will generally produce a horse that is attractive. Attractive horses, other things being equal, will usually sell for higher prices than unattractive horses. A good horseperson will understand that good nutrition is simply grooming from within. Added to this, keeping your horse sound and physically fit will also increase the value.

One should remember that all buyers should request that an equine veterinarian examine virtually every horse that is to be purchased. There may be X-rays involved and even some bone scans. The healthier your horse, the more likely he is to get a good report from the examining professional.

In this day and age, it is also likely that a top-class professional trainer in your horse's discipline will be asked to examine and maybe even ride the horse in question. The healthier he looks and the happier he seems, the more likely it is that you will get a favourable report from the buyer's professional.

When preparing a horse for sale, it is also a good idea to have your farrier get the horse in the best shape possible from the standpoint of hoof health. Making sure that shoes fit well and appropriate angles are maintained will go a long way to assist you in properly presenting your horse to potential buyers.

Each of the elements that I have addressed in this answer is key to elevating the value of the horse. Get his competence high in his discipline, and then present him in the best way that human hands can achieve.

Recommended additional resource: 11

Question 41

Monty, do you believe horses are emotional or am I right in simply treating them by the book with exactly the same procedures for every horse?

Answer

Before answering this question it is necessary to define exactly what you mean by 'emotional'. The *American Heritage Dictionary of the English Language* defines emotion as 'a strong feeling as of joy, sorrow or hate – a state of mental agitation or disturbance'. The dictionary goes on to define 'emotionally' as 'of or exhibiting emotion – readily affected with emotion'. Given these definitions, then it is my opinion that the horse is a mixed bag. I believe that he can be in a state of mental agitation or disturbance. I do not believe that he is capable of much sorrow or hate.

Once we have established that horses can certainly display some forms of emotion, we should accept the fact that horses are reactive. They will respond to the actions of individuals in their presence. It is unlikely that they stand around feeling sorry for themselves or ponder about individuals they might hate. These emotions are reserved almost exclusively for humans. It has been established that some primates will openly grieve. I believe that very little of this type of emotion enters into the lives of our horses when dealing with their human counterparts.

If we are to be successful at creating good relationships with our horses, then we must establish a shift away from the traditional methods of training through extrinsic measures (violence). It is difficult to expect optimal performance from an animal that is doing his work because he is afraid not to. Just as with people, horses will give you their best performances when they are working because they want to. There are opportunities to learn more about the nature of the horse in the 'Recommended Additional Resources' section at the back of this book.

Recommended additional resources: 1, 4, 6, 12, 13, 14, 15

Question 42

Dear Monty, How can I get my horse to want to work cattle? I look forward to your response. Thanks!

Answer

One can only encourage your horse to want to work cattle. There is a clear genetic pattern where certain families display a greater tendency than others to want to work cattle. Once you have a horse that is willing to move with the motion of the cattle, then it is up to the trainer to create an environment where the horse likes his work.

In my textbook, I have written about causing the horse to be happy to perform. This psychology is applicable to all phases of training your equine student. One must allow the horse to have fun, no matter the task at hand. I have often told the story of how I create an environment in which young horses learn to work cattle while having fun with it.

Study the fundamentals of the cow work as professed by the most successful trainers you can learn from. Information is available on this subject from world-class trainers. One should never take the position of 'making' the horse work cattle, but always operate on the basis that you cause your horse to 'want to' do his work.

Horses have a tendency to habituate so as to follow moving objects. I recall in the 1960s being called to Hawaii to judge a major horse show. I met a trainer there who had moved from California. This man trained in many disciplines: jumping, Western, cutting and even trick routines.

He had customers who wanted him to train and create competition cutting horses. There were very few cattle available for this use. So he developed a system that looked like the old-fashioned clothes-lines of the inner city, the ones where the ropes were on wheels and people could pull the clothes to and from the house from the windows. On one end of this crude contraption he put a bicycle, which was fixed in place. He took the front tyre off and replaced it with the rope, so that he could put an assistant on the bicycle that would move the rope using the pedals. Then a pillowcase was fixed to the rope so that it could be moved back and forth across one end of his working area.

He called it a mechanical cow. I thought it was one of the silliest things I'd ever seen. It was my opinion that no horse would learn to work a cow by training on a pillowcase. Was I wrong! Now, fifty years later, there's every kind of mechanical cow that you can imagine, even ones remotely controlled by the rider in the saddle. This crude device was certainly no substitute for the full range of activity required of the cutting horse. It did, however, fulfil the primary need for the horse to move with an object simulating the behaviour of the stalking animals.

Horses never cease to amaze as they adapt to different conditions. It is down to us to observe their behavioural tendencies so that we can give them the best chance of reaching the goals we set out for them. Following these principles, the knowledgeable horseperson will realize that pain and pressure will produce a resentful horse and workings with the horse's own nature is apt to create a willing partner.

Recommended additional resource: 1

Question 43

I recently got a new Quarter Horse that I adore! So far, we seem to be adjusting to each other well. He moves beautifully, and I am excited about the upcoming show season to see how we do together. The only problem is that he swishes his tail when I ask him to move forward. What does this mean, and do you have any advice on how to make him stop?

Answer

Swish-tail horses bother me a lot. I am not a fan of horses with this habit because my study of the nature of the horse has revealed to me that, while dogs wag their tails when happy, horses swish their tails for the opposite reason. When I see a horse swishing his tail, I am certain he is not happy performing the tasks that are being required of him. Once the habit is in place, it is very difficult to overcome.

Some horses are born to be swish-tails. That's not something I often say about problems I meet in remedial work, but I believe that, while rare, it does occur. I also believe that there is a genetic link when it comes to the tendency to swish tails and that this feature is often the property of females rather than males.

Since swishing the tail is a gesture of disapproval, it may well be a response to pain. Such pain could arise from many different sources. Inflamed joints, an abscessed tooth, a hoof bruise or even a bit that your horse finds inappropriate can cause pain, which in turn may become manifest in producing tail-swishing.

One of the most often-detected producers of pain in the ridden horse is an ill-fitting saddle. These can create sores or invisible hot spots, which may be extremely painful to your horse. Once back pain causes tail swishing, the habit is established. Take care because in this way one can cause a chronic psychological condition that may persist even after the source of the pain has been eliminated.

Decades ago I formed the conclusion that single-line lungeing was the second worst piece of horsemanship on earth – second only to striking a horse to inflict pain. The act of single-line lungeing compromises the horse's anatomy and tends to create inflammation throughout the skeletal system. Joint pain is one of the primary causes of the swish-tail condition. One should be ever mindful of the recommendations that I make for alternatives to single-line lungeing.

My recommendation to you is to take the pressure off your horse as much as possible. Never consciously cause the horse pain, and be patient with your approach to training. Take care not to overmatch your horse on any given day, which may result in an attitude of resentment. Even after executing these recommendations, be prepared to live with less than total success, because this is truly a hard habit to overcome.

Experience has taught me that humans' attempts to communicate with their legs cause horses to swish their tails far more than other forms of communication. Spurs are a great contributor to the swish-tail condition. My organization has created, at my request, an object called the Giddy-Up rope. It is my version of a painless whip. It will assist greatly in stopping a horse's desire to swish his tail while increasing forward impulsion.

It would be a good project for you to acquire some videotape of dressage competitions. Observe these wonderful horses as they give their utmost in an effort to reach perfection in the dressage discipline. Watch, however, how the swish-tail phenomenon often increases greatly with the piaffe.

The piaffe is a manoeuvre that is trained by the use of spurs while holding the horse firmly so that no forward progress is achieved. There is a mixed message here, and one that is executed with spurs playing a major role. Swishing the tail is virtually certain to occur under these conditions.

Observations of this phenomenon have caused me to state on several occasions that, if it were up to me, I would eliminate the piaffe from dressage routines. It is not up to me, and I am not directly involved in the dressage world. However, it is clear to me that very few horses are happy while executing the piaffe. I have seen the piaffe executed with minimal discomfort and a seemingly happy horse; my point is that it is extremely rare.

Recommended additional resource: 1

Question 44

How do you cure a barn sour horse?

Answer

With patience and consistency. Basically, you have trained your horse to be what we call 'barn sour', and it will take a lot of work on your part to re-school the horse's thoughts about returning to the barn. Horses are reactionary animals: their actions are the result of the techniques we have used.

You might insist that you didn't train your horse to be barn sour, but if you have ever ridden your horse back to the stable, dismounted, untacked, tucked the horse in a stall or box and given it food and water, then you have trained the horse to be barn sour. If you have done this as a consistent pattern, and many horsepeople have, then you have created this problem without observing its presence.

Now that you have strong evidence of what caused this problem, a significant shift in your pattern of behaviour is absolutely essential. From now on, don't ride back to the barn to do all those things. Stop before you get to the barn, dismount, and loosen the saddle and walk – leading your horse to the barn. Better yet, ride past the barn, stop, dismount, scratch your horse's neck under the mane, talk and enjoy a few quiet moments . . . *then* turn and lead your horse to the barn. Let the horse stand for a while before removing the saddle and blanket, receiving any feed or turned loose. Make the 'end of the day' reward occur somewhere other than at the barn.

Vary the routine to keep it from becoming boring or something the horse may begin to anticipate as he used to anticipate 'charging' back to the barn. It will be fun for you and particularly for your horse to work your way through the 'barn-sour' syndrome. View it as an opportunity to learn more about good horsemanship and enhance the relationship with your horse.

The 'Recommended Additional Resources' section at the end of this book includes educational products that address the issues of barn-sour horses, separation anxiety and napping, baulking and/or refusing to leave the barn. If you choose to become familiar with these lessons, your knowledge will assist you greatly in your effort to correct the barn-sour condition.

Recommended additional resources: 1, 7

STARTING AND JOIN-UP

With an understanding of the horse's language and nature, one can begin to learn the concepts I have come to call Join-Up. This section will help you to become aware of the most often asked questions regarding this wonderful act of partnering with a horse for a common purpose.

Join-Up is the title I have given to the collective body of work that I have extracted from nature itself. This title comes from a moment in time when one can witness the horse choosing to be with me rather than away from me. This phenomenon is accomplished through the use of the horse's language, which I have called the language of *Equus*.

The Join-Up process is the centrepiece of my effort to cause a horse to accept its first saddle and rider. The traditional world of horsemanship has known this process by the term 'to break'. I don't consider my process properly referred to with the word 'break'. I don't break anything, and I much prefer to think of that process as starting rather than breaking.

The language of *Equus* is one of gesture and not of sound. The world is rapidly becoming familiar with the notion that horses do communicate, both with each other and with other species, including human beings. It is my position that this language has been in existence for millions of years and that we have just been too busy with our own world to take the time to observe the world of the flight animal.

Through a prescribed series of gestures, I demonstrate that the horse makes a choice to be with me, and once that happens, accepting the first saddle and rider follow on logically. I have been demonstrating for more than twenty years now that this process can occur, through these methods, with far less stress and anxiety than the traditional methods, which normally include pain and restraint.

Question 45

I attended a four-day clinic at Flag Is Up Farms to become familiar with your techniques and have been starting all of our babies

successfully now for six years. Recently, we have b~~
Sport Horses (ISH) in addition to o~~
discovered that the ISH does not
instinct. The problem that I now ~
exhibit all four signals within a co
usually without even cantering. I c
initially, but it can be difficult to kee
them, which then makes them leery
they will Join-Up and follow, but not ~~ ~~ ~~ave
exhausted the flight instinct. I have e~~ ~~mented with moving on to
saddle, rider, etc. more quickly, but have found that mentally they are
not really ready for this either. I believe this is due to the fact that I
have a less than successful Join-Up.

Your method has worked really well, and we have produced many
lovely riding horses as a result, so we hope that we can transfer this
process to our ISH babies with as much success.

Answer

I am pleased to hear that these methods are working for you and
especially that you are producing champions. I suppose it's possible
that you are worrying about things of lesser importance than you need
to. I work with many ISH on my tours, and I find them to be quite
normal within the realm of *Equus*. If I have a horse that is exhibiting
lower flight tendencies than I am comfortable with, I will often use a
plastic shopping bag on a long bamboo cane to increase the flight
response. When I feel I have what I want, I simply toss it out over the
fence and proceed without the bag. You might try this, but it sounds
like you are doing well as it is.

It is commendable that you are working to improve your
relationship with your horses and to understand their nature better. I
am certain that as you add numbers to your experience bank you will
look back at this question with a chuckle. The problem you cite is
certainly not one of deep concern, but I find it interesting that you
place importance on the breed you are working with.

Certainly there are differences as we journey through the many breeds of equine the world has to offer. However, it is my opinion that the similarities far outweigh the differences. I find the ISH to be a wonderful breed. They are filled with athletic ability and generosity as well. Because of their heterozygous background, they are blessed with what the geneticists would call hybrid vigour.

Without going into a full genetics lesson, let me briefly explain to you that Thoroughbreds, Arabs and other breeds that have existed in a pure form for prolonged periods of time (centuries) have a more consistent gene pool and are termed 'tending toward homozygous'. Geneticists agree that the purer forms of any particular breed possess less hybrid vigour than those of a more recent origin, which are more 'tending toward heterozygous'.

The Warmbloods of the world, including the Irish Sport Horse, are the result of recent out-crosses to mix the bloodlines of the cooler draught breeds with those of the established Thoroughbred. These horses tend to have a more vigorous physiology. They will generally have healthier feet and stronger bones than the older breeds. They also tend to have a more laid-back attitude. Psychologically as well as physically, they are generally less fragile than their purebred cousins.

The ISH is extremely intelligent and highly trainable. If we get it right with these horses, they will become exceptionally gentle and are often great mounts for the children of the horse world. I encourage you to continue to work with your ISH, and I believe that you will ultimately return to me with reports of great successes.

Recommended additional resource: 1

Question 46

I just bought a Tennessee Walking Horse that was used by you years ago to teach a clinic. I have had no training and feel I need to 'catch up' with my new friend. Where would you suggest I start?

Answer

It's great to hear from old acquaintances! I am pleased that the Tennessee Walking Horse is once again OK for people to own and ride. As you are probably aware, the Tennessee Walking Horse industry has been under great pressure because certain individuals have chosen to use inappropriate and painful techniques to achieve an action from their horses which scores high in the competition ring.

No Tennessee Walking Horse has broken the rules. It is people who have broken the rules. The Tennessee Walking Horse is a fantastic breed that produces a comfortable ride over long distances and leaves its rider far less likely to be muscle sore than horses of traditional gaits. The Tennessee Walking Horse typically has a wonderful character and is truly suited to family leisure riding.

England, Germany, South Africa and Australia are the fastest growing areas for the Tennessee Walking Horse outside of the US. It is gratifying for me to see this breed regaining its popularity. I am working hard to assist the breed association in coming up with humane solutions to the problems that have beset its industry over the past fifty years or so.

Congratulations on your choice of a wonderful mount. I am sure you will have years of pleasure from that decision. I look forward to a time when Tennessee Walking Horses are seen in abundance along the roadways of the UK, as they have so much to offer the leisure rider.

I recommend that you use all of the websites available with respect to the Tennessee Walking Horse breed. There is www.twh bea.com as well as many chat rooms and forums that are filled with information regarding either the latest news and regulations of the breed, or just details on pleasure riding. I think you will be pleased to see how much is out there regarding the flat-shod Tennessee Walker.

Good luck with your journey to become a better horseman.

Recommended additional resource: 1

Question 47

When you start a Join-Up with a horse, won't they think they have done something wrong? What does the horse think at that moment?

Answer

If you are referring to the point when you send the horse away, remember that it is the horse's language that you are working in. When this gesture is thought to be offensive by a human being, it's because the human is attempting to translate it into our language. I have borrowed this gesture from the world of the wild horses, just as I have the whole lexicon of the language *Equus*.

Horses are perfectly comfortable speaking the language that they have always known. Watch the horse at the end of the Join-Up, and you will realize that nothing negative has resulted from your sending the horse away. It is virtually impossible to draw a horse back to you until that horse is away from you. What I am attempting to do is to set up an environment whereby the horse exercises freedom of choice.

Don't try to speak two languages at once. Learn the language *Equus*. The student horseperson is best served by working with a great number of gentle horses. The novice can, in fact, get into a lot of trouble with the raw, untrained juvenile. If a student makes a series of mistakes, it can take long periods of time to regain the trust of the untrained horse.

Many scientists have written about the behaviour of flight animals and how they respond to the actions of other species. The flight animal is quite accustomed to fleeing to avoid what it perceives as danger. In the wild horse herd, it is commonplace for adolescents to be sent out of the family group for periods of time as discipline for unacceptable behaviour. It is a part of their culture, and they understand it quite well.

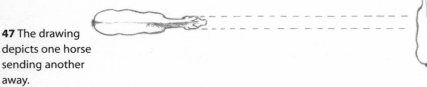

47 The drawing depicts one horse sending another away.

Anyone who chooses to study my concepts closely will realize that I wait until the horse chooses to make a move to leave me. In the absence of this flight response, I suggest adding to the gestures to flee gradually until the desired response is achieved. It is at that time that I respond by overtly sending the horse away. I try not to be terribly aggressive in this action. I make a concerted effort to match my movements to the sensitivities of the horse with which I am working.

Once the animal has reached his flight distance, the tendency is for him to communicate with me a desire to return. It is at that point in time that I observe the four gestures that I have written about so often. Once I have received them, I assume a passive position, thus inviting the horse to return to me. If he does, it is my responsibility to congratulate him with a good rub and gestures of welcome and understanding. Short of achieving that response, I work in arcs or semi-circles in front of the horse, and if I get my language right, Join-Up will happen.

With these procedures accomplished, one can begin a relationship with the horse whereby he understands that coming closer to the human is a good thing, while distancing himself from the human is less than a good thing. It is important to note that the negative consequences of doing the less than good thing are to return to work. Too many horsemen would strike the horse for going away, thus producing a relationship of anger and distrust.

You may see some practitioners using whips to drive the horses away from them, and then stopping the whipping, backing up, eyes on eyes, drawing the horse towards them. This procedure historically has been termed 'whip breaking' and was used by the motion picture industry to achieve stunts they termed 'in liberty'. I am not a proponent of this type of training. I do not believe in striking a horse to achieve any response.

Recommended additional resources: 1, 3

Question 48

I've used Join-Up several times over the last couple of years with my now five-year-old gelding. I've actually used it with my horse both to improve my body language, our communication and relationship, and as a 'punishment' when his playful mouthing turned into a nip. I'm just wondering if he knows the difference.

Answer

I am pleased that you are learning to do Join-Up and using it successfully with your horse. Yes, it can be used to improve your body language and your relationship with your horse.

Join-Up is the language of the horse, and therefore he does not concern himself with the reasons for your actions. He will judge you only on the moment in question. I commend you for the thought process that has taken you through the scenario you have outlined in your question. It is unfortunate that too many horsepeople deal with their animals without considering factors that you have taken seriously.

Sending the horse away is a very good method by which to set up negative consequences for unacceptable behaviour. However, we must be careful not to create a full Join-Up scenario each time we perceive the need for discipline. If we experience repeated negative behaviour, then in my opinion we should move to create negative consequences more specific to the moment of negative actions.

To give an example, suppose a horse walks right into your space and uses his head as a battering ram to knock you sideways. If we send the horse away, work him hard and then invite him back in again, it could very well be a good idea. If the horse repeats this action, this would call for a specific procedure to reduce the impulse to flee.

In my work, this scenario would have me reaching for my Dually halter. I would attempt to set up an environment very similar to what it was when I experienced the bad behaviour. When this action was repeated, I would then school by repeated stopping and backing up using the Dually halter to create cooperation. I would repeat this negative consequence until I noticed a distinct change in the behavioural patterns of my horse. I have confidence in the Dually halter and what it will do, so I know that, properly used, it will be effective.

In summary, when something isn't working, change it. Don't keep repeating the same pattern and expect the outcome to change. With horses, we often need to be more immediate with our discipline. We must remain aware that they think in the moment. It's worth repeating here that we need to operate within the guidelines called 'PIC/NIC', standing for Positive Instant Consequences and Negative Instant Consequences – in this context with emphasis on the word *Instant*.

Recommended additional resources: 1, 3

Question 49

How important is it to provoke the horse to move at speed during the Join-Up process? Is it imperative for the horse to canter and bring his adrenaline up high for the Join-Up to be effective, or could I complete a Join-Up in walk and trot if the environment is not suitable (i.e. round pen too small for horse to canter comfortably)?

Answer

Let me answer your question by first stating that I don't like the word 'provoke'. One should be communicating to get flight, not necessarily provoking. Next, I would like to say that speed varies greatly with size and breed. One can do Join-Up at a walk with a tiny pony or a massive draught horse. However, most breeds will respond to the flight communication with some degree of speed. It is not necessary for the horse to canter for Join-Up to be effective. It is also not necessary for adrenaline to be high.

One should keep in mind that when carrying out Join-Up as a starting process, most horses should feel the saddle while cantering. With most breeds, it is dangerous for the horse to canter with the rider up before he canters carrying a saddle. If one's round pen is too small for the horse to canter comfortably, then you must not canter. If the round pen is too small for the horse to canter comfortably, then it is also too small for the starting process.

Recommended additional resources: 1, 3

Question 50

Do you always ask horses to follow you around at the conclusion of the Join-Up session?

Answer

In the past few years and with the encouragement of Crawford Hall, who worked with me for over twenty-five years at Flag Is Up Farms, I do it on a regular basis. Mr Hall has come to call it 'quality time', and we believe that it is quite helpful in creating a horse that is content with his work. I am certain that there are no negative consequences to this, and it can only be helpful.

It is possible that your question inquires as to the percentage of horses that follow me around during this quality time session. It seems to me that it would be something like 99 per cent. I say only because I am sure that there were horses that were less than 100 per cent willing to follow me during this time, but I can't remember the last one to do this.

Following me during 'quality time' is simply the expression of acceptance, whereby the horse believes that I am a partner and not a slave owner. If I have done my work properly, there is a strong likelihood that the horse will take this position. Students who achieve less than a good Join-Up and are still a bit tentative with their communication skills may find it a little more difficult.

Having outlined the above factors, let me say that whether the horse follows the trainer or not isn't terribly important. It is wonderful when it happens, and if the student is working with a genuine effort to achieve it, it will eventually happen. Horses are too pure in their instinctual behaviour to fail this test when it is presented properly. They are happy to have a friend and generally expressive when it happens.

Question 51

How does one apply the Join-Up method without a round pen?

Answer

The round pen is not the critical factor in applying these concepts. It is a convenient place in which to work. Should you use a square pen, horses will tend to 'stop down' their energy in the corners. If you take a square pen and panel the corners off, you effectively create an octagon. This nearly round enclosure will work very well. If you choose to work with horses in a wide-open space, their natural tendency will be to work in very large circles, and you must be in very good shape to go the distance with them.

There are several other questions dealing with round pens. Make yourself aware of my recommendations for round pens in my textbook.

Recommended additional resource: 1

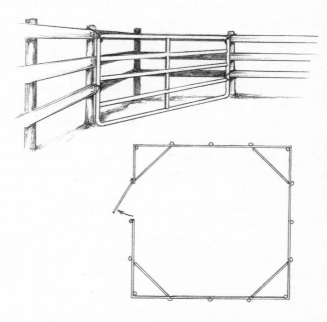

51 A square pen with the corners removed.

Question 52

Is Join-Up effective for older horses that have been trained by traditional methods?

Answer

Absolutely! I have a long list of older horses formerly trained with traditional methods that were then brought to me with what seemed to be insurmountable problems. Lomitas, Prince of Darkness, Barlet, My Blue Heaven and many more were re-trained using Join-Up and went on to become champions. Some horsepeople maintain that my methods will eventually be better known for their effect on remedial horses than for their effectiveness with raw ones.

As I do demonstrations worldwide, I work with approximately four remedial horses for each starter that I deal with. I accomplish Join-Up with all of them. Often I see a marked improvement in the remedial horse's behaviour with nothing more than Join-Up accomplished.

Several times in my career I have set out to deal with one remedial problem or another only to find that, after Join-Up, the problem disappeared. I recall receiving a phone call one day from a trainer who had a horse at a California racetrack. He told me that the stewards had barred the horse from training there and asked me if he could send him to Flag Is Up Farms for remedial training.

He explained to me the horse had become so anxious to do his morning workouts that he would just go mad as he entered the track itself. He would rear and buck, usually dislodging his jockey, and then run dangerously among the horses already at work. Racetrack stewards take a dim view of this action, and they ruled him off.

When I received the horse on Flag Is Up, he seemed quite normal in every way. He was quiet and cooperative – just a brown horse. The next day I did Join-Up with him and spent a significant amount of time getting him comfortable to be with me. On the second day I took him to my training track. He did nothing wrong. I called the trainer, who said that the vanning company must have dropped off the wrong horse. As his all-over brown was a far from distinctive colour, I could see that this was a distinct possibility.

It turned out to be the right horse, and after about a month of training reinforcement we sent him back to the trainer at Santa Anita. He went on to have a successful career, never causing a problem after that moment. Granted, this is an extreme case of Join-Up acting as the full solution, but it is amazing how many horses dramatically improve with nothing more than the Join-Up process.

Recommended additional resource: 6

Question 53

Is it possible to do Join-Up with other horses around?

Answer

If there are other horses visible while doing Join-Up, it is a distraction. We should strive to give our horses the best chance to understand what it is that we're trying to impart to them; so, wherever possible, you should do Join-Up with as little confusion around as possible. If necessary, however, Join-Up can be accomplished when there are significant distractions. Remember that I do about approximately four hundred Join-Ups per year with an audience present. Nearly all of them are done in a see-through round pen. So my horses deal with major distractions. Since Join-Up has been 100 per cent successful for more than seven thousand horses when done in front of audiences, I maintain that you can overcome distractions. Nonetheless, because I have done tens of thousands with and without audiences, I am well aware that it is easier to do Join-Up without distractions.

I have accomplished Join-Up while within a herd of horses, all in the same enclosure. I have also managed to get good Join-Ups with as many as four horses at a time in the round pen. However, these exercises are pushing the limits and are not particularly easy on the horses or the horseman.

For Join-Up, I consider a round pen 50 feet (16 metres) in diameter, with a good fence and appropriate footing, to be ideal. If the round pen is placed so that the horse sees no other animals while you're working with him, so much the better. If the environment can be arranged so that the horse cannot see anything moving outside the pen, that it is also desirable.

Question 54

How often do you do Join-Up with a horse?

Answer

I do the full complement of Join-Up in my operation four, five, maybe six times and that is all. After that you live by the concepts of Join-Up for the balance of the horse's life. This means that when you go into the loose box, you do not just walk in, grab hold of him and pull him around. You walk in, and when he moves away, you look him in the eye, square up, and move towards him while being sure to stay out of his kick zone. When he looks back at you, you walk away and let him catch you.

One cannot simply drop the language of *Equus* into your brain, any more than someone could miraculously and instantly cause you to speak French. It's a long process and not something someone can teach you overnight. There is a process for learning it, and the potential is available to you.

In my textbook, I inform the reader of all of my recommendations in the use of Join-Up through the process of bringing your horse through the months and years of training. It is critical that we become familiar with the needs of our horses in the processes whereby we come into a partnership with them.

In performing Join-Up, it is critical that we use the language *Equus*. Obviously, before we can use it, we must learn it. In that same textbook, there is a chapter on the language. It is comprehensive and detailed. Using these two chapters will give you a full understanding of not only how to do Join-Up, but how and when to use the correct language.

Recommended additional resource: 1

Question 55

Why is it important to start a horse in thirty minutes?

Answer

Since I began to publish books on my work, our office receives approximately a hundred questions a week from horsepeople worldwide. This question often comes up among them; so here I will attempt to put it to rest once and for all.

It is not important to start a horse in thirty minutes. I start a horse in thirty minutes in my demonstrations because this allows the audience to watch the full process without having to wait hours and hours, even days or weeks, to see it completed. I often say that if the process is effective enough to complete in thirty minutes, then it is a good demonstration for public audiences. I tell the people present that if they choose to take a week to do what I do in thirty minutes, that's fine. I go on to say that I much prefer to start the horse after a few days of preliminary preparation.

Dr Robert M. Miller of California and Rick Lamb of Arizona combined their talents to publish a book in 2005. It is called *The Revolution in Horsemanship and What It Means to Mankind*. Dr Miller is a world-renowned equine behaviourist and has studied my methods for more than ten years. In the early trips Dr Miller made to Flag Is Up Farms to watch me work, I remember he advised me strongly against emphasizing the fact that horses would accept saddle and rider in about thirty minutes, because this assertion was attracting too much criticism. He said that the fraternity of horse trainers felt I worked too fast and that the process would be confusing to the horse, or that the lessons would be quickly forgotten. I respect Dr Miller, but I continued to answer by saying that the horses seemed to set their own pace and finish their sessions with a good attitude.

In his recent book, however, Dr Miller outlines how, through Join-Up (using the language *Equus*), this procedure can effectively be done in thirty minutes with far less stress than is incurred in using traditional methods.

Over the years he has come to recognize quite clearly that what I was suggesting to him is absolutely true. When a teacher lingers over lessons with young children, one can readily observe boredom set in. I recognize that teaching is an art form, but the good horseperson will move lessons along, keeping the horses' interest and watching them learn.

In the course of starting horses at home, I go through the mouthing and long-lining processes for a week or so before we actually put a rider on. It is an easier transition for the horse and safer for the people as well. When I do a demonstration, the only way I could duplicate this process is to ask the owners to execute these procedures at home before bringing their horse. As you might imagine, this would be impossible. I wouldn't know whether it was done at all, let alone whether it was done properly. I have no contact with the owners before the demonstration, and I believe that's the way it should be. I certainly could not send people around to do these procedures, as this would create an immense amount of criticism that the horse was already trained by the time it came to the demonstration.

As it is now, people say it looks too easy, and some critics will state that the horse was already trained, even when we work hard to maintain a separation between my organization and the owners. If I somehow could complete these early procedures before each of the demonstrations, most of the people present would believe that the horse had been ridden before. It is my hope that horsemen will complete mouthing and long lining before they start their horse. If they learn and use Join-Up properly, they too will come to know how easy it can be.

There are some individuals who think that it is a trick and so they investigate this work in a negative way. Some will even say that I use medications to help in the starting process. This is absolutely untrue, as every demonstration owner knows. Anyone who understands horses will quickly realize that no medication is used. I am strongly opposed to the use of medications in attempting to train horses in any field. I do not believe that it is effective and, if I did this without revealing it, it would be totally dishonest.

It is my hope that the information I have given here more clearly defines the time required to start horses, and that people everywhere will be able to learn more about the techniques of working with horses in the absence of violence and force. If they practise these techniques, I believe they will have more fun with their horses, and the horses will be happier and more successful.

Recommended additional resource: 1

Question 56

I want to start my horses in thirty minutes, but I don't get the same results as you do. What should I do?

Answer

Join-Up will save you so much time that you will be well ahead even if you take several days before your horse willingly accepts saddle, bridle and first rider. What is important is the quality of the work, not how fast you accomplish it. By quality, I mean the level of acceptance and understanding the horse shows regarding the Join-Up goals. We all want well-behaved, happy and willing horses. It is on this that you will be judged, not on the amount of time it took.

When I do my demonstrations, it is critical that I use the time to educate my audience to the greatest degree possible. I almost always tell the viewers that if they choose to take a week to do what I do in thirty minutes, that's fine. I go on to say that if I took a week to do it, the audience wouldn't be very comfortable in those buildings I do my demonstrations in.

Don't be too critical of yourself if it is taking a bit longer than you had hoped to accomplish your goals. Each horse that you educate will, in fact, educate you. Observe your horses as you work, and let them show you by their responses what works best for you.

It is a fact that if you work with many horses that are already trained, it will improve your performance. One does not have to deal with raw horses all the time. Putting many trained horses through Join-Up, saddling and long-lining will cause you to work in a smoother and more efficient manner. Then, when you encounter a raw horse, the work with it will be easier given your accumulated experiences.

Question 57

Mr Roberts, in your first book, Join-Up is described as quite a long process with negotiations between horse and horseman. You describe signals from the horse and the human. Today it is a short process taking just thirty minutes. What has changed?

Answer

It is difficult for me to understand how you came to this conclusion. My first book was published in 1996 and my fourth book in 2002. The Join-Up procedure is described briefly in my autobiography of 1996. In my textbook Join-Up is described in detail: there are pictures and drawings and a lot of words, but the process described is essentially the same.

In 1989 I visited Queen Elizabeth II at Windsor Castle. I demonstrated Join-Up for Her Majesty on twenty-three horses. It took approximately thirty minutes on average for each horse to accept its first saddle, bridle and rider. Since that first English demonstration trip, I have done Join-Up with more than seven thousand horses in front of public audiences. The time taken on each has averaged approximately twenty-seven minutes.

In 1952 I started approximately one hundred and fifty horses using Join-Up. A large percentage of those were mustangs. I don't recall timing them, but I can say categorically that the procedure has remained relatively stable for all of the fifty-odd years since. I hope I have improved and, in fact, I am sure that I have learned to be smoother and more efficient. However, I can assure you that the procedure today is essentially identical to what it was in the 1950s.

Recommended additional resources: 1, 4

Question 58

When you cause the horse to run a quarter of a mile, is that not tiring him out before he drops his head? Is he dropping his head because he's tired?

Answer

I am pleased to have the opportunity to answer this question. It crops up too often to disregard. The fact is, however, that it is a question without good foundation. By that I mean that it rests on certain assumptions that are invalid.

The first is the assumption that I cause the horse to 'run' a quarter of a mile before looking for gestures of communication. The fact is that, with the average horse, more than 70 per cent of the time is spent at a trot. The canter, in a 50-foot round pen, is rarely any faster than a slow canter and not a run or gallop.

What we have, then, is a horse that has travelled a quarter of a mile, trotting for approximately 400 yards/metres and cantering for approximately 40 yards/metres. The effort outlined would be comparable in human terms to a person walking steadily for about three minutes. I think it is fair to say that virtually any sound horse could accomplish this effort well before exhaustion was a factor.

In no way do I want my horses to be exhausted. Exhaustion would be counterproductive to creating a willing partnership with the horse. When a horse is exhausted, it tends to be resistant to learning and fearful of human contact.

Lowering the head is totally unrelated to physical exhaustion. It is a gesture that the horse performs willingly and with some degree of relaxation, not of fear, stress or exhaustion. If you work through Join-Up with twenty to thirty horses, any idea that exhaustion plays a role will disappear. Give it a try, and I think you'll be surprised with the results.

Recommended additional resource: 1

FEARS AND PHOBIAS

The questions I have selected for this book have been gathered from several separate sources. Probably the greatest number has come to me during my demonstration sessions. I typically spend about an hour and a half during each of my evening presentations answering questions from the audience. These are written out on 3- by 5-inch cards and read to me, in many cases by an interpreter.

Tens of thousands of individual cards have been handed in. As you might imagine, however, many are duplicates. In fact, most of the questions will fall into a range of fewer than one hundred. I don't believe that any other clinician has the global exposure that I have. It has been amazing to see the similarity of problems people have with their horses worldwide.

One factor that I have found quite surprising is that horsepeople tend to feel that their problem with their horse is unique. While there may be slightly different aspects in certain cases, I am of the opinion that the solution is virtually identical across all the various instances of the problem. Most of the time, it matters very little what the breed of the horse is, what colour it is, or even the sex involved. If you have the problem, you need the solution.

As I read through the thousands of questions, it became clear that the largest category could be entitled 'Fears and Phobias'. So it seemed sensible to give the title to a section of the book and draw the solutions together so as to reduce repetition in the answers that I give.

To begin, then, I need to list the most often mentioned fears and phobias horse owners have brought to me. In recent times, our culture has created certain objects that are new to the world of horses and thus constitute something they should be frightened of. Probably the newest item on this list is 'the little plastic shopping bag'. Ironically, the existence of this item has actually afforded horsepeople the opportunity to use in their training a scary object that has very little chance of directly causing injury to the horse. This means we can use this item to assist us when dealing with fears and phobias in general. Once we successfully eliminate one phobia, we are well on the way to helping our horse with any phobia.

Here, then, is the list of the objects of 'fear or phobia' that most often crop up in questions put to me:

1 Little plastic shopping bag
2 Trailers (floats and horseboxes)
3 Walking through water
4 Clippers
5 Cattle
6 Birds
7 Pigs
8 Sheep
9 Bridges
10 Applause
11 Chainsaws
12 Fireworks
13 Marching bands
14 Bicycles
15 Motorbikes
16 Lawnmowers
17 Umbrellas
18 Balloons
19 Tarpaulin

For the purpose of this section, I have chosen to deal with items that horses have a tendency to be inherently frightened of. There are many items within the horse industry of which horses have very little inherent fear but of which they often, justifiably, acquire a fear. Whips, twitches, farriers and aggressive men would probably head this list.

The number of questions regarding phobias of an inherent nature runs into the thousands. The solutions are far fewer and quite similar. In order to understand how to deal with fears and phobias, it is important to know that horses, as flight animals, are meant by nature to be frightened of anything of which they are unfamiliar.

Most horsemen are aware of the fact that virtually all horses are frightened of pigs. Horses don't get to see pigs very often. They smell funny, sound strange and move in a way totally unfamiliar to most horses. Given all of this, any self-respecting flight animal has to get the heck out of there when it sees a pig.

Horses raised on pig farms are virtually never frightened of pigs. Familiarity without pain breeds acceptance. This is a premise absolutely essential for the horseperson to understand if they are to be effective at dealing with fears and phobias. It is our obligation to create familiarity in the absence of pain.

Horses are not inherently frightened of whips, but after pain is produced with this object then fear sets in. What we must do to overcome the fear of objects on our list is to allow the horse to see and feel this scary thing repeatedly without feeling any form of pain from it.

Having understood these fundamental points, one can begin to work with the horse, using my recommendations, and expect positive results in a relatively short period of time.

First, though, I would recommend achieving a good Join-Up with every horse that has a phobia to be dealt with. One might accomplish three or four good Join-Ups and so create a horse willing to follow you around and happy to be in your presence.

Then, with a good Join-Up in place, I recommend schooling with my Dually halter until the horse knows the value of standing still and remaining with you. It is very difficult to deal with fears if the horse blasts away from you at every exposure.

These basic procedures will create a foundation on which you can work to deal with the fear in question.

Question 59

If I'm riding my horse near trees or hedges I must be very careful to watch for plastic bags. If my horse sees one fluttering in the breeze, he wheels and runs in the opposite direction. It is dangerous, and I have no idea what to do.

Answer

Regardless of the phobia targeted, the plastic bag can be a great tool for us in our effort to eliminate the fear. I have found it effective to use a light bamboo cane about 8 feet (2½ metres) long. The ones I use are about ½ inch (12 millimetres) in diameter and light enough for a small lady to handle with ease. You can typically buy these inexpensively at a garden centre.

A plastic shopping bag can be attached to one end of the pole using a rubber band to secure it. A second rubber band can encircle the plastic bag to hold it close to the pole, so that it doesn't fly around in the breeze.

I start out by simply scratching the horse all over his body with the end of the pole that has no plastic bag on it. The plastic bag is on my end of the pole and under my arm.

59 The plastic bag can be first presented while strapped down with rubber bands and then gradually opened to add to the challenge.

Working with the pole, I touch the horse until he accepts it anywhere I want to stroke him with it. When I see the horse relax, I take the pole away. If the horse tends to be frightened and elevate his adrenaline, the pole must continue to approach him. He soon learns that the way to get the pole to go away is to relax.

When my horse is standing perfectly comfortable through the procedures involving the bamboo pole, I then reverse the pole and repeat the process with the end covered by the lashed-down plastic bag. When the horse accepts this end of the pole, then I remove the second rubber band and allow the plastic bag to float freely. This will generally evoke a fear response. I use the same technique of taking it away when he relaxes and bringing it towards him when he is tense.

When my horse will stand with one little floating plastic bag, then I attach four, five and six plastic bags to the same end as the original one. I work to achieve complete relaxation while these bags jump up and down on the back of the horse, rub under the belly, down the legs and even from the chest up to the jaw stroking the throat of the horse.

If my horse is frightened of birds or things above him, I do a lot of elevating the plastic bags, flying them above his back, and then bouncing them down onto his hips, back, withers, neck and even the top of his head. When the horse will stand for this procedure, you are well on your way to eradicating fears and phobias of all kinds.

Remember that the Dually halter is there for schooling should the horse try to blast away at any point in this process. If you feel as though you're getting into trouble, it is appropriate to back down to a level that is attainable, and then once more work towards those procedures that the horse finds difficult to accept.

At this point, one can begin to target the particular phobia at issue. Obviously we have by now dealt with the little plastic bag and have begun to eliminate the fear of birds coming from above. Now it's a matter of creating familiarity with the objects listed above.

Recommended additional resources: 1, 5, 13, 14

Question 60

I've had my horse for three years, and if I want to take him somewhere I have to ride him or lead him. He refuses to go into a trailer (horse box) or truck (lorry).

Answer

The procedures for dealing with loading horses in the trailer or truck are set out in detail in my textbook. Over the course of my career I have now dealt with well over two thousand difficult loaders in more than twenty countries.

Once you have accomplished the procedures I have outlined above, you will be well on the way to dealing with loading problems successfully, as the Dually halter work has been done. Follow my recommended procedures and the problems of loading will be a distant memory.

While the Dually halter is a major part of the solution to the loading problem, please also refer to the 'Loading' section of this book for a more extensive answer to this question.

Recommended additional resources: 1, 5, 9

Question 61

My horse will not allow you anywhere near her with clippers. If they are running, it's impossible. If they are quiet, you can come close but not touch. What can I do?

Answer

A useful approach to dealing with a horse that has a fear of clippers involves desensitizing to a hairdryer. Your horse will become familiar with the sound of an electric motor, feel no pain from it and actually enjoy the warm air it produces.

When answering this question in demonstrations, I advise people to give the horse a bath and then dry the animal off with a hairdryer. It is a good idea gradually to direct the flow of air towards the head, ears or wherever the fear of clippers is evident. This procedure will be effective for head-shy horses as well.

Once your horse is standing quietly while the hairdryer is producing a flow of warm air into the ears, you are ready to begin to massage the ears with one hand while you handle the hairdryer with

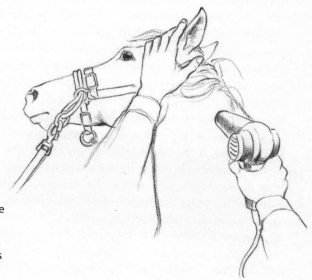

61 The motor noise and warm air from the hairdryer will desensitize the horse, making using clippers much easier.

the other. The next step involves recruiting an assistant to deal with the hairdryer while you do the clipping.

With the Dually halter assisting you, it is important to remember to back up to an acceptable area of work any time your horse becomes resistant to what you are doing. Make your transitions slowly. Respect for your horse is essential, and they have a right to test all of these actions as you move through the recommended procedures.

Recommended additional resources: 5, 7

Question 62

Please help us with horses that are frightened of birds and animals.
We ride on the roads in our community and many of our horses are
phobically frightened of such animals as cattle, birds, pigs and sheep.
What do we do?

Answer

Many stories have come to me, particularly from the UK and Europe, regarding horses that have a fear of cattle. This can be very dangerous. Many horsemen have reported suffering serious injury from horses that wheel around and bolt, throwing them to the ground.

Once again, it is very helpful to have the preliminary work with the Dually halter in place before tackling this particular problem. Then, I recommend borrowing a calf (generally an orphan) from a cattle farmer. They will generally be very happy to have someone else feed their calf for a few months. Once you have this baby on your property, then you can begin to create a familiarity for your horse with the sight of cattle and, more importantly, the smell of cattle.

It is advisable to place the calf at a fairly substantial distance from your horse at first. Gradually move the calf closer and closer until the horse is accepting the sight, sound and smell of this animal. Horses will usually fall in love with a calf within a month or so, and after three or four months they will be perfectly happy to walk down the road with cows following just over the fence.

Birds have been relatively well dealt with during the plastic bag

ASK MONTY • MONTY ROBERTS

procedures described above, but if there is the need to de-sensitize to birds further, you can even work with the plastic bag and the pole while riding. Just be very careful and be ready to throw the pole away if your horse takes great offence at the plastic bag waving ten feet above its head.

Stories about pigs frightening horses abound in the horse industry. Apart from those horses raised on pig farms, there is just about one story for every encounter. Once again, call upon a pig farmer to loan you a cute little squealing pig and follow the same procedure that I recommended with the calf. It often takes longer with a pig, but the process will be just as effective.

The sight of a woolly sheep running across a green field can drive some horses into a frenzy. The sound of the sheep is foreign to the horse, and the smell is right off the charts. I bet you can guess what I am going to recommend. Go find an orphan lamb, and by the time that lamb is woolly, your horse will love it. Go easy at first and watch familiarity become fascination.

Recommended additional resources: 1, 7, 14

Question 63

I belong to a club that has been formed for the purpose of getting together periodically for rides through the countryside. There are forty people in our club. About thirty of them will attend any given ride. We constantly have to deal with horses that have fears of various objects and sounds that we confront on a day's ride. Please assist us in recommending procedures so that we can advise our riders what to do with their horses between rides. Help!

Answer

For the next group of fears and phobias, I will tackle together a large group of objects and sounds that are typically frightening to horses.

It is my opinion that the auditory phobias are best dealt with by playing recordings of the troublesome sounds, which you can put on a continuous loop in your stable. Many such recordings are now available. You can set the volume quite low at first, and even place the speaker well away from the horse. Gradually increase the volume and bring the speaker closer. I have used this method, and it really works. Virtually any sound that drives a horse crazy can be dealt with using these recordings.

For the visual challenges, I suggest the procedures I have already recommended in this section. Introduce the objects slowly and safely. Do not overmatch your horse or place him or yourself in a dangerous position. Each time your horse stops and relaxes even slightly, take the object away. Use the same general procedures that I recommended with the plastic bags, and you will see results fairly quickly.

I have done demonstrations with many objects, some of which also make frightening sounds, and experienced very good results in thirty minutes' work, with great help from the Dually halter. After doing Join-Up, I could get my horses to follow these scary objects around the round pen.

You don't have to accomplish this in thirty minutes. Follow the outlines I have given you in this section, and you should have fun

63 The drawing shows using a ridden horse to assist in the process of walking through .water.

ASK MONTY • MONTY ROBERTS

causing your horse to be more cooperative and safer than he was when you began the procedure.

Sometimes you may have to go out looking for the problem, rather than bringing it to the horse, for example, bridges. Bridges produce frightful images. Shadows, deep pits and funny sounds all work to produce phobias within the world of horses. I recommend that, having already made your horse familiar with the Dually halter; you start out with a single piece of plywood (4 feet by 8 feet or a bit more than 1 metre by 2 metres). Place it on the ground and, using the Dually, school your horse to walk over the plywood with ease.

Once your horse will negotiate the sound and the sight of the plywood, then begin to select bridges, beginning with those that are the least frightening and working up towards those that are the most frightening.

Stay safe, make your transitions to bigger challenges as gradual as you are comfortable with, and be willing to drop back to an easier level if your horse becomes fearful. Try to find bridges with safe footing. Don't hesitate to lead your horse, even from the back of another, if you don't feel it is safe to ride during the training process.

When your horse will walk quietly across bridges, the next step is to be sure that he will cross through what is under the bridge! Often it is a small stream or body of standing water. Many horses are frightened of testing the bottom and refuse to go in at all, let alone quietly walk through it.

The fact that the Dually halter work has been done will help greatly in dealing with the fear of walking through water. This procedure will require the use of a gentle riding horse that is willing to walk through water.

Recommended additional resources: 1, 3, 5, 7, 14

Question 64

I was at a horse show with my five-year-old Warmblood. It was his first time away from home, and I intended to compete in a novice dressage class. Everything was going fine until we experienced a brief rain shower. With that, someone saw fit to pop up a brightly coloured umbrella. I was thrown to the ground, and my horse stormed back to where I had parked my car and trailer. Since then, I can't go near anyone with an umbrella. A child with a balloon is essentially the same thing to my horse. He goes ballistic at the sight of either one of these objects. Please somehow let the world know what we should do to overcome this phobia.

Answer

One of the best demonstrations that I ever did was in Munich. It was with a beautiful Warmblood called Nubie. He had a long history of injuries to himself and people resulting from his phobia regarding umbrellas. It is true that they are awful objects for horses to deal with.

Once you have accomplished Join-Up and Follow-Up (where the horse simply follows the trainer in the round pen as a display of trust), and established work with the Dually halter and the plastic bags, the umbrella becomes a much easier prospect than you might imagine. Keep it folded up for a while, gradually open it and stroke your horse with it, keeping your transitions quite gradual.

Having completed all of these procedures, you will be walking around holding the umbrella up over your horse's back within a very short period of time. You will be able to open and close it rapidly without great disturbance to your horse once he realizes that it is not an object that produces pain.

The Dually halter will prove to be the difference between this procedure and many others that horsepeople have tried. Once the horse has accepted the Dually, training to these fearful objects becomes a much easier process, as your horse will feel he can't blast away from you and go ballistic.

Balloons are just a simple transition from the plastic bag. One can even put the balloons on the pole and use them in the same way you used the plastic bags. The squeaking of the rubber might produce an added dimension, but your horse will deal with that very quickly.

Recommended additional resource: 1

Question 65

I keep my horse at livery. My boarding stable uses plastic tarpaulins to handle the muck from the stable. My horse hates tarpaulins. I think I should change stables because it seems he might injure himself before he becomes accepting of these awful objects. Is there anything I can do to cause my horse to be more accepting of tarpaulins?

Answer

Fear of tarpaulins can be dealt with in just the same way as fear of walking through water or over bridges. Instead of the plywood, use a large tarpaulin lying on the ground. This procedure can even have an educational effect on the process of loading into a trailer. If you are diligent in applying the procedures I have outlined here, causing your horse to walk over a plastic tarpaulin will be an exercise in simplicity.

65 The drawing depicts the use of a ridden horse to assist in walking over tarpaulin.

If you have read this entire section on fears and phobias, you are by now prepared to deal with these problems more effectively than most of the horsepeople of the world. You will notice that I have not mentioned the word 'whip' or given any cause for raising your voice. One should stay focused on the fact that keeping your horse's adrenaline down is of key importance.

Staying safe and making your transitions slowly will have a great deal to do with how successful you are with these exercises. Remaining observant of your horse's responses and being quick to back down to an acceptable level is equally important in ensuring success in your efforts to alleviate fears and phobias.

Recommended additional resource: 1

Question 66

My horse refuses to walk under tree limbs while I am riding him. The branches are often not low, but he still refuses to walk under them if I am on his back. He has no trouble walking under them if there is no one on him. Sometimes I have to get off him in order to pass under them. Can you help?

Answer

This is a problem that I have worked with in demonstrations several times. First I did Join-Up and schooled to the Dually halter. After that, I began to loose school the horse in the round pen. On one side of the pen I placed a structure that my assistants had made for me. It was a rectangular frame, constructed out of 2-inch (5-centimetre) PVC water pipe. The frame was is about 4 feet (about 1½ metres) in width and 9 feet (3 metres) in height, creating a doorway with an opening that a horse could fit through.

It was easy for each of the horses I worked with to learn to pass through this narrow place. If it is difficult for the horse, it might be necessary to put panels as wings on the side of the frame towards the centre of the pen, so that the horse is less likely to duck around it. Work until the horse passes through this object quite willingly.

Next, attach some strips of plastic tape to that top of the frame, and at first roll them up and hold them in place with a rubber band. As your horse learns to handle the plastic strips, gradually lower them until he has to duck his head to go under them. You might initially have to separate the strips at the centre to give him a bit of a passageway allowing him to learn that it's OK to go through there.

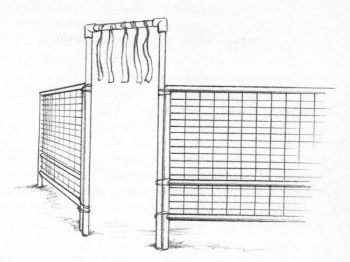

66 The PVC pipes and panels create a passageway. The strips of plastic can be extended and this arrangement can be used first without a rider and then with a rider.

Once this is accomplished, saddle your horse and put him through the same procedure with the saddle on. If you are not comfortable riding through at this point, put a mannequin rider on your horse and let him pass through it dozens of times, sweeping the plastic strips across the mannequin as he negotiates the narrow passage.

Typically, within thirty minutes I have a rider on my horse going first in one direction and then in the other, back and forth under the plastic strips with little or no fear that any harm will come to him. You will find this a very effective way to deal with the fear of passing under tree branches.

Question 67

My horse, Figaro, is scared of cows. Do you have any advice of how we can help him to overcome his fear?

Answer

Fortunately, I had the opportunity in October 2004 to work with a horse that had a phobic fear of cows. It happened to be in the north of England, in a small village called Osbaldeston. I did Join-Up with the horse, and it went well. After Join-Up, I schooled the horse to the Dually halter so he would respect the lead. When I had full control of the horse, I asked my assistants to open a door about 50 yards away and to bring in a young cow by the name of Poppy that had been trained to lead and was quite well behaved.

My horse was at once a bundle of nerves and clearly wanted to bolt right through the side of the round pen. I put Vicks, a popular decongestant remedy with a strong menthol scent, in the nose of the horse to reduce the smell of the cow to a minimum. Once the Vicks was in place, I had only the sight to contend with. I began by asking my assistant to turn the cow away from my horse every time the horse looked in the direction of the cow. I was creating a Join-Up of sorts between the cow and the horse. I worked for approximately thirty minutes and ended up with the horse calmly following the cow around the round pen.

Horses are frightened of things they are not familiar with. It turns out that this horse had been scared by a group of cows in a field, and its reaction had caused injuries to both itself and the rider. Since that time the horse had been terrified of the smell or the sight of cows. Once the horse was satisfied that the cow wasn't going to hurt him, he accepted the animal comfortably.

There is a humorous side story to this particular experience. The horse in question was owned by a lady who had recently divorced, and had moved with her children and horse to the countryside. When she rode down the roadside, her otherwise wonderful mare went ballistic whenever the neighbour's cows came into view.

It turns out that the dairyman on that neighbouring property was also recently divorced. When the horse's owner contacted my team, we asked if there was any chance that the neighbour had any cattle trained to lead. It turned out he did; so, when my owner brought her horse to the demonstration, the dairyman brought along the beautiful yearling heifer I mentioned above, Poppy.

We worked with these animals together, as I have described, and it was quite obvious that the neighbours were becoming more and more friendly throughout the course of the evening. It was a cold night in

Osbaldeston, and I noticed them sitting closer and closer together, sharing a blanket. I feel certain that I have created a situation whereby this lady can now ride her horse over to visit a very friendly neighbour – something she never could have done until we dealt with this phobia of cows!

You can have fun with your horse dealing with these challenges if you get your work right. There is no reason to act violently in any way. It is absolutely imperative that you raise the level of trust within your horse in order to overcome fears of this nature. In this case, after doing a normal Join-Up, I simply did Join-Up with a cow, and it seemed to work out very well.

Question 68

I have two young horses turning five; they are both afraid of water and of being bathed. I have avoided trying to force water on them and wonder what you do to get them to the point of bathing without fear. I am afraid of making them more nervous than they already are, so I haven't done a lot to this point. What is your recommendation for dealing with this?

Answer

I answer this question quite often. Remember that a horse can stand out in the rain without any problem: it's only when water hisses from a hose under pressure that many of our horses take fright and try to avoid the water to get away from the sound.

I tell people that if they have a spare stall that they don't mind getting wet, they should put the horse with the problem in it. Then get a stool or a table so you can reach over the wall while holding your hose. Have a pistol grip on the hose and start out with a fine mist. You may have to direct your fine mist to a point away from the horse initially. Slowly bring the water closer to the horse, possibly just touching the legs at first. Work gradually upwards until your horse is actually standing in a misty shower-like environment. Proceed by lowering the direction of the water once again, and then carefully cause the flow to be a slightly more direct stream rather than the foggy mist.

The point here is to show the horse that there is no pain connected to the water from the hose. Remember that the horse and all flight animals are built by nature to be frightened of anything with which they are not familiar. Once you have familiarity, it is likely you will lessen the fear. Our obligation is to create these conditions with no pain to the animal.

When he will stand reasonably comfortably for this procedure, then you can move on to the next step. Open the door slightly, put the pistol grip through it and begin to spray the floor all around the horse. Gradually work up the legs and onto the body as he becomes relaxed with the process. If you choose a good hot day, your horse will probably love it in a matter of ten minutes or so.

Having accomplished these steps, then you can begin to direct the water to sensitive areas: the head, under the belly and up between the hind legs. You will have fun with this if you carry out your procedures through progressive steps that your horse can handle.

SNORTING AND SENSE OF SMELL

It is appropriate to move from fears and phobias to a section on the incredibly sensitive olfactory (smelling) system that horses possess. We humans have no idea how to assess the incredible abilities of horses to smell over vast distances. Learning about their sense of smell is an important part of becoming better informed about what our horses are thinking.

The act of smelling involves inhaling actual particles of the substance itself. These microscopic cells are floating on the breeze. As an animal inhales these particles, they pass over what is known as the olfactory plate. These microscopic portions of the substance involved strike the plate giving off the essence of the substance involved, so that the animal can process and identify the characteristics of the smell itself.

We human beings generally think we have an acute sense of smell. The fact is that our olfactory system is less than one-hundredth as effective as that of the horse. We are all familiar with the incredible powers of the bloodhound to follow a scent, and we've become familiar with the use of many breeds of dog to find people under collapsed buildings or illegal drugs in baggage at the airport.

Dogs are a wonderful example of a creature with extremely sensitive smelling apparatus. Horses, however, are also extremely well equipped to process and identify certain smells. They know that we are meat-eaters, if we are, and they are able to smell water from miles away.

A key part of the horse's olfactory system is its rather large olfactory plate. When we hear a horse snort, it is clearing off that plate so that drifting particles of a given substance can stimulate the system. Thus snorting usually occurs when the horse is seeking to identify potential danger.

Question 69

My horse is never hard to catch, or overly nervous, but he snorts, a sound I have never heard from a gelding. We have all kinds of wildlife

*around the farm. Sometimes we ride in a group and he sounds off
and gathers all the riders' attention. What is he trying to say?*

Answer

I have a very strong idea of what he is trying to say. Horses have essentially the same senses as we humans: sight, taste, touch, hearing and smell. When we smell, we inhale particles of a given substance. Then our brain kicks in to determine what the substance actually is. We can certainly identify such pungent substances as lemon, vinegar and many foods that we have come to know.

Horses conduct the same tests as humans in this area of olfactory exploration. But horses have an ability to smell many times greater than that of a human being. While the horse's sense of smell may be less powerful than that of the bloodhound, it remains absolutely incredible how acute it really is. We humans find it difficult to imagine the awesome abilities of certain animals to smell with sensitivity unimaginable in our world.

When a horse senses danger, there is a tendency for it to clear off the olfactory plate, as it may already be coated with several layers of smells. One of the ways of accomplishing this task is to blow air across the olfactory plate in such a way that it produces a snorting sound. Some horses are louder and more expressive in this tendency than others; usually, the wilder they are, the louder they are.

The aura of particles secreted from reproductive areas of other horses are sometimes met with the act of a horse curling the upper lip up and blowing through the nose, clearing out the olfactory system. While this is essentially for the same purpose, the fear of confronting a predator will usually get you the snort and not the lip curling.

It is probably fair to say that when a horse snorts he is saying, 'I need to get to know that smell better. I must learn who has produced that smell. It seems like a predator to me, and I must investigate thoroughly before allowing this individual to get any closer.'

Recommended additional resources: 1, 7

Question 70

How can I help my horse? He hates any kind of strong smell, like fly spray, rubbing alcohol or vinegar, and he won't let you near him enough to begin de-sensitizing him. I am not looking forward to the problems of dealing with getting my horse used to these smells.

Answer

I have used automatic sprayers that dispense insecticide and fragrance to de-sensitize any horse that has this particular challenge. A quick search on the Internet found an appropriate product on www.horse.com, but I imagine your local feed and tack store may also carry an automatic dispenser that would work.

It's best the horse doesn't see you place the dispenser high up in the box stall, as he should not associate you with the sound or odour. The procedure is to auto-dispense the offending aerosol (automatic dispensers are available at DIY stores) every fifteen minutes until the horse becomes oblivious first to the sound and then to the odour as well. This may take a few days, or it may happen much sooner, depending on the horse. Reduce the interval between sprays gradually until the horse is no longer bothered by the procedure.

Once this has been accomplished, you should have little problem with spray bottles or aerosol cans. As always, I recommend introducing any de-sensitizing exercise gradually. In the case of automatic spray mechanisms, they should first be placed well away from your horse and then gradually brought closer as the response dictates. If you observe a dangerous anxiety level, move the mechanism away until the response is moderated, then begin to bring it closer again.

SEPARATION ANXIETY

One of the fastest-increasing remedial problems in today's horse world is separation anxiety. It seems to me that with properties becoming smaller and horses being kept more closely confined, their sense of bonding becomes more acute. It is incredible how much more frequent questions about separation anxiety have become, even in the single decade since my first book was published.

It is well for us all to remember that horses are herd animals. They find comfort in the safety of a family group numbering at least ten and often over thirty. We humans tend to assume that a horse will be just fine all on its own. In doing so we are ignoring one of their most basic needs.

When we take the time to learn the nature of the horse, and its language too, we begin to respect the needs they have. They are basically fearful of anything unfamiliar to them. Being alone means that they are vulnerable to predators without the protection of the family group. It is understandable that this adds to the fear that they might be killed.

Question 71

How do you cure a herd-bound horse? I have a horse that is so bonded to two other individuals that I can't take him away from them. I can't ride him to other locations, nor can I even put him on a trailer to transport him. He goes crazy.

Answer

When I was gathering the material for this book, it became apparent to me that separation anxiety was a far greater remedial problem than I ever imagined. I would estimate that variations on this question have come to me more than five hundred times in the past two or three years alone.

Horses are herd animals. Some horses are in more deep need of constant company than others. The horse that is perfectly happy while solo is rare. In the case of your horse, it seems that there is an intense desire to be in an environment with a companion.

If your horse panics when his buddy horses leave the property without him, he is a herd-bound horse subject to separation anxiety and needs to be de-bonded. A horse that goes crazy when its companions are away is a danger to itself, others and property. Separating your horses from one another gives them the opportunity to learn they can survive by themselves. If you have a small property and separation is not possible in your circumstances, you have other options.

Join-Up is an effective way to cause your horse to want to be with you. This, in effect, is part of the de-bonding process. When your horse is comfortable in your presence, he is less likely to be stressed in the absence of other horses. In rare cases, I have seen horses change dramatically after nothing more than a good Join-Up. It seems that this procedure tends to say to them they are safe. Spending quality time with your horse is part of the answer to this ever-increasing problem called separation anxiety.

Once a good Join-Up has been accomplished and your horse is completely at ease with you, then you can bring into play another aspect to solving this problem. Borrow a friend's horse. Agree with a friend that you will 'trade' animals for a short period of time, during which you will take care of their horse while they take care of yours. Another thing you can do is let your horse spend some time in a different location. Simply shift your horse around for a while.

The de-bonding process will not take long. Once it has been accomplished, make use of the horse's new attitude by periodically introducing various new individuals into his life so that he accepts this kind of change rather than feeling a constant need to have specific horses around him and going ballistic when they aren't there.

A good horseperson should realize that overly bonded horses that are subject to separation anxiety create a danger to themselves and to those who work with them. We should also realize that it is far more difficult to enjoy a relationship with a horse that is herd-bound than with one that is comfortable about being removed from his friends whenever you choose.

One must realize and accept the fact that a time commitment, probably quite a substantial one, is going to be necessary in dealing with a horse such as yours. I enjoy these types of challenges, but then I guess it's only fair to tell you I have been accused many times of being maniacal in my desire to understand better the workings of the equine mind!

Recommended additional references: 1, 3

Question 72

I cannot break my Thoroughbred mare's habit of fence pacing. The moment she loses sight of company, she goes crazy and paces the fence. She is very insecure. I am at a loss as to how to break this habit. The fence is electric. I have dotted hay nets around the place, which was suggested by a friend as well. I am very close to being kicked out of my grazing because of it. Can you help?

Answer

Horses are herd animals. Some horses are in more deep need of constant company than others. The horse that is perfectly happy while solo is rare. In the case of your horse, it seems that there is an intense desire to be in an environment with a companion.

While it is quite possible that this individual requires the company of another horse, often a different species will do. I have seen horses settle and become friends with sheep, goats, calves and donkeys. I even remember a Thoroughbred trainer who had a horse that simply had to be with his pet parrot.

The nervous characteristics of the individual you describe will probably respond quite well to being provided with a friend. The art of creating a reasonable relationship with your horse is more likely to be challenged by over-bonding than it is by under-bonding. Horses such as yours are a challenge, but, like difficult children, they can be a lot of fun to deal with at the same time.

While it may be difficult to comprehend, I believe that when we have a better relationship with our horses they become a good deal more settled in their attitude. In rare cases, I have seen horses change dramatically after nothing more than a good Join-Up. It seems that this procedure tends to say to them that they are safe. They seem to realize that the world is not out to get them, and become far more tranquil as a result. Since this can do the horse no harm, I recommend it even if the chances for improvement are relatively slim.

PULLING BACK

This section deals with a remedial problem that is proof positive of how intensely horses feel driven to go *into* pressure instead of moving away from pressure. I liken this tendency to children that are teething: they want to bite on hard rubber – before that was available, mothers would given them branches. We humans have this tendency only in the mouth; horses have it over their entire body.

The reason we want to bite on something when there is pain in the mouth is just another indication of how clever Mother Nature is. We lived for many centuries without the benefit of dentists or painkilling remedies. If we tended to back away from pressure in the mouth when we felt pain, we would simply have starved. Survival of the fittest set us up to go into pressure when experiencing pain in the mouth.

The horse is a prey animal. One of the primary predators of the horse is the canine family, and dogs tend to attack horses in packs, some of the pack distracting the horse while the primary attacker would generally go for the soft flanks. If the horse were to flee while being bitten, the flesh would be ripped away, probably with fatal blood loss. Mother Nature's answer was to give the horse the impulse to go into the attacker and then attempt to kick him away.

The horse that pulls back today is simply expressing these inherent tendencies. The human will tend to view the act of pulling back as an illogical response that serves no purpose. If we are to be good horse-people, we will adopt the position that everything the horse does makes sense. We just have to search out the basis for his actions.

Question 73

Every time I tie my mare up she sits down until she breaks either the halter (headcollar) or the lead rope. How can I stop this? She stands still most of the time for me to groom her, but not always. She is a wonderful horse and very smart, usually.

Answer

Virtually everyone who has owned a horse has at some time experienced an episode where the horse pulls back when tied. If your horse successfully breaks free several times, she is likely to develop a phobia where she feels compelled to pull back when tied. Certain activities are more likely to evoke pulling back: loud, sudden noises, or movements in the horse's environment, or tying the horse in the trailer with the back door open.

Horses are naturally 'into-pressure' animals; the behaviour your mare is exhibiting is to move into the pressure she feels on her poll. Your goal is to re-train her to yield to pressure without causing unnecessary pain or fear. I would suggest your first step should be to school her with the Dually halter until she is comfortable moving off the pressure.

Having completed this, you will need a solid, smooth wall, 8 feet (about 2½ metres) high and 24 feet (8 metres) wide, with a tie ring in the centre of the wall at a height of approximately 7 feet (2 metres).

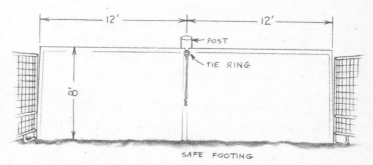

73.1 This indicates the wall of the area designated for dealing with the pull-back horse.

Attached to the tie-ring you must have a thick bungee rope (such as 'The Leader', available through www.jedlickas.com; or check with your local tack shop or farm supply to see if they stock it). The next step is to create a D-shaped enclosure with round-pen panels attaching to either end of the wall and curving to meet approximately 10 to 12 feet (3 to 4 metres) from the wall at the centre point.

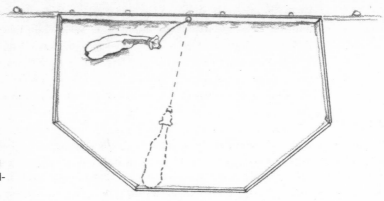

73.2 Overhead view of training area for the pull-back horse.

73.3 The panels come in to play to keep the horse safe.

Take your mare into the enclosure, attach her headcollar to the bungee rope and exit, closing the round-pen panel after you. If your mare chooses to pull back, the bungee rope will stretch approximately 10 feet, at which point she will bump her hindquarters on the panels and be unable to go further back. The bungee rope will continue to exert a gentle pressure on her head until she steps forward, releasing the pressure. She is in a safe environment in which she can experiment with the pressure and learn to move forwards and accept being tied.

The environment I have briefly described for you is depicted in great detail in my textbook. Horses that pull back can be extremely dangerous as, when they panic, they can hurt themselves and others. It is imperative to keep yourself safe and create a safe environment for your horse.

Recommended additional resources: 1, 7, 15

Question 74

My horse is fine with almost everything I do. I can tie her up for grooming, but I cannot tie her in the trailer while I go round to close the ramp. She pulls back and breaks everything. She has injured herself twice, and now I don't put her in the trailer at all.

Answer

If you have put your horse in the trailer and tied her up without first closing the trailer behind her, you have broken the number one red-letter rule in horsemanship. I am assuming that you didn't know about this rule before you made this mistake. If this book does nothing more than help people through this one problem, I will consider it a success.

It seems that I need to address this issue on every page of every book that I write. I know of so many injuries to both people and horses from this one mistake that they are too numerous for me to count. Virtually every city I visit has a casualty incurred by tying a horse in the trailer before it is secure from behind.

Typically, people will ask, 'Well, what do I do then? If I go around to the back without tying the horse, he will back out before I can secure a gate behind him.' There is no excuse; you can't do it. Once we accept this red-letter rule, then we can deal with the options available that are safe.

The first and easiest option is to have a friend present to close the back while you hold the horse in place. This will allow you to be flexible on the lead instead of frightening your horse by tying it up firmly in a narrow place. Once your friend has closed the back, then you can make the tie with no problem.

The second option would be to use a driving line. Run it out through the front of the trailer and then walk to the rear, holding the horse as you go. This will again allow flexibility instead of a solid tie. Once you have closed the back, then you can return to the front to make the tie secure.

Another option would be to leave a cup of grain in the manger of the trailer. This will generally keep your horse busy for at least the ten to fifteen seconds that it takes to secure the rear of the trailer before returning to the front to make the tie. Anticipating and eating this snack usually becomes a pleasurable experience, eventually causing the horse to be quite easy to load and tie.

Every horseperson should remember that *there is never an excuse for tying the horse in a trailer before the rear is secure*. No circumstance is worth the risk of injury or death to horse or human. Even in the absence of physical injury, breaking this rule is apt to create psychological damage that will cause your horse to fly back out of the trailer when the door is opened instead of backing out comfortably.

Recommended additional resources: 1, 3, 9

WILD AND DANGEROUS

What would a question-and-answer session be without inquiries about how to handle a horse that is wild and dangerous? Mustangs have provided me with some of the most entertaining and gratifying sessions of training that my career has known.

Any time we are dealing with an animal that is large and fast, it can be dangerous. When we add 'wild' to the scenario, then we multiply the danger factor significantly. If we take the time to become familiar with the needs and fears of the horse in question, we tend to reduce the danger.

My time with the wild mustangs was not only fun but also extremely educational. The untouched horse approximates the mustang no matter where you find him on the globe. What is helpful to those of us who choose to work with the untouched horse is that all horses are extremely similar psychologically speaking, and they mean us no harm.

Their similarity allows us to learn about all horses when we learn about any horses, and the fact that they mean us no harm is great comfort to those who might fear for their safety. Mother Nature seemed to know exactly what we human beings needed when creating the horse.

Question 75

I have an untouched horse, and I am in big trouble. My question is 'How do I get a halter (headcollar) on an untouched horse? HELP!'

Answer

I love working with these horses. We are currently building a new 'untouched horse' facility as a part of our school here on Flag Is Up Farms in California. We have many courses that deal with the untouched horse as a primary part of the lessons offered.

A chute (crush or small enclosure) is very helpful when it comes to putting on the first headcollar. This structure is made up of planks or metal pipe tubing with spaces between them. These spaces are large enough for an artificial arm to go through so that you can stroke the horse while standing outside the chute. There should be steps on the outside so that you can stand in a position where you can reach the head and neck over the top of the chute without placing yourself in danger. Once in this small enclosure, we ask the horse to accept a lot of touching and rubbing with our human hands. I also recommend the use of an artificial arm, as described later in answers about one-sided horses and horses that are difficult to shoe (see Questions 79 and 80). I rub them with this arm all over their body, under their belly and down their legs.

Having accomplished these procedures, I then begin to touch the horse's head and neck and introduce him to the halter while he is standing in the chute. There is a logical process to be followed after the first halter has been put on. This is well covered on the DVD *You and Your Wild Horse*. It is crucial that one stays in a safe position at all times while working with untouched horses.

Ian Vandenberg and Kelly Marks work together as instructors in my concepts in England. They have devised a clever system that uses a forked stick with a hook on it to put a halter on an untouched horse. It is quite something to see and very effective.

Recommended additional resources: 1, 13, 15

Question 76

I recently purchased a rising two-year-old Thoroughbred that I would like to start with the idea of eventually racing. He is nicely bred and extremely well conformed. This colt has a high level of energy and has had very little handling. When I got him home to my stable I found I was in a lot of trouble. He is wild and dangerous. It is very difficult even to catch him in the stall, and he can whirl and then kick with a volatility I have not seen. I need help.

Answer

I would like to answer this question by giving an example, as your experience sounds quite similar to a recent experience of my own.

During my October 2006 visit to England, I was in daily contact with the English office that is in charge of arranging my tour, selling tickets and attending to all of the details of the demonstrations. Shaun Whelehan is a member of the office staff and has been a great asset to the English team for about five years. At that time Shaun happened to have a girlfriend, Ashley Horton, who rode young Thoroughbreds for Mark Usher, a racehorse trainer.

Shaun mentioned to me that Mr Usher had purchased a yearling colt named King Alchemist – the most expensive acquisition of all the yard's 2006 purchases. He also told me that Ashley was in charge of the starting process for all of the youngsters that were getting on for twenty months old – and, with some anxiety in his voice, that while all of the others had gone well, King Alchemist was a very scary proposition.

King Alchemist was reported to be very leery of humans, so that at any point might strike with a front foot or lash out with a hind one. It was said that there was no chance to put a saddle on after the first attempt, at which he went straight over backwards with the saddle and then bucked and kicked, managing to get the saddle under him and tearing it to pieces.

When I arrived at the Usher stable, I found a beautifully conformed youngster that was suicidal and psychopathic. I cannot remember ever seeing a young Thoroughbred that was more dangerous to handle than King Alchemist. I must say that Ashley was brave even to go into the box and put a headcollar on this colt. What I saw was beyond belief, and I am sure would have resulted in grave harm to either Ashley or the colt had I not been called in.

An interesting aspect to this story is that I had a block of three free days – Tuesday, Wednesday and Thursday – at the end of my English tour schedule. The only reason I had these days was that a meeting had been cancelled by an unrelated party. My next stop was the Netherlands, where I had a sold-out venue, and it was imperative that I was there on time.

Adrien Maby is a young Frenchman who accompanied me on this tour as a potential rider. Adrien and Ashley managed to get King

Alchemist to the round pen where I initiated my work. I accomplished Join-Up in a relatively short period of time. This part of the procedure was relatively normal. Touching him anywhere but on the head, however, was met with utter disapproval. After Join-Up I chose to treat King Alchemist as a remedial, spooky horse, and I carried out the procedures appropriate to that assessment.

The Tuesday session was approximately three hours long, with two or three rest and water breaks for each of us. I mentioned to Adrien and Ashley on the first break that I was hoping to achieve a score of ten on Thursday afternoon. I told them that ten would mean that I could saddle King Alchemist, drive him on the long lines and put either of them on him in the round pen. For the purpose of this report, I will state that by the end of Tuesday's work I estimated that I had reached a level of two out of the targeted ten.

On Wednesday I was able to start at approximately the same level of accomplishment that I had reached on the Tuesday. After another three hours, I felt that we had reached a level of about seven out of the targeted ten. I went to bed on Wednesday night far more optimistic than I had on Tuesday.

Thursday was a day delivered to me straight out of heaven. King Alchemist picked up right where we had left off, and within one hour on that day I had saddled and long-lined the colt and allowed each of my riders a chance to ride him in the round pen, walking, trotting and even briefly at canter. With my ten tucked away, I went off to Holland the happiest man you could imagine.

Mr Usher has reported to us since that week that King Alchemist is actually doing better than any other of the rising two-year-olds. He is working on the gallops as the leader of his group of freshman racing prospects. It is my hope that we will see his name on the international list of stakes winners when he is mature and ready for competition. King Alchemist was an extremely educational experience for me, calling on every nuance of my experience in order to achieve my ten.

It should be noted that while Ashley was a brave girl and a good rider she was without any education in my concepts. It was Join-Up and Follow-Up that allowed me to gain a level of trust essential to reaching my goal. King Alchemist was responsible for providing a test for my concepts and they proved to be successful.

Recommended additional resources: 1, 14

Question 77

Are there horses that are so called 'man-haters'?

Answer

I get this question approximately five hundred times a year. Each time I'm asked, I say that it is no surprise when a horse loves a woman and hates a man. This is not rocket science: a man has abused the horse. Horses don't make these things up. They act out only as a response to what others have done to them. I probably work with two hundred horses a year that have been abused by men.

Recently, in Ohio, a mare was brought to me by her owner. He also happened to be her farrier, and said it was impossible for any male farrier to deal with her. This owner went on to admit that he had tied the mare's legs with ropes, put the ropes over the beams in the barn and pulled the legs up so that she couldn't kick. This is abuse, and there is no other name for it. We worked with the mare, and in the end she allowed me to handle her legs with no problem.

If you have a horse that hates all men, stop and say to yourself that the horse has a right to its response. Then learn my methods, put them to work and watch the horse regain trust. We should not demand that any horse gives us its trust until we earn it. Trust is not something that any horseperson can require of a horse; it is for the horse to give trust freely. Human relationships are very much the same. Trust is not something that parents can demand from children, nor can a child demand trust from a parent.

The act of trusting someone is clearly the property of the individual who chooses to trust. It comes about only after a period of time has elapsed in which trust comes to seem appropriate. With these tenets clearly in view, it is easy to see that trust is a condition virtually impossible to obtain when there is violence connected to the relationship. This is true whether the relationship is horse-to-human or human-to-human.

'Violence' is defined as physical force exerted so as to cause damage, abuse or injury. The word 'violent' is defined as marked by or resulting from great force or having shown great emotional force. Within these definitions, it is clear to me that words can hurt as much as whips can, so one should not ignore the violence of emotional conflict. Yelling at a horse or child or acting in a threatening fashion can result in the perception of violence.

Why should we question the fact that a horse might recognize a male as being more likely to produce violence than a female? Isn't it likely that most horses that are physically abused suffer these acts at the hands of a man rather than a woman? I suppose it is fair to answer the question by saying that no horse is born a man-hater, but that some may have learned to hate men because of abuse they have experienced.

Question 78

Why do you feel that 'sacking out' is an undesirable training technique?

Answer

The first part of my response to this question is that we need to settle on an agreed definition for the term 'sacking out' before taking a stand on it. The process called 'sacking out' takes on several different forms as you travel around the world. Even in the United States it will appear as one thing in New England and quite a different process in New Mexico. Nevada will regard 'sacking out' in one way, while Florida will employ a process significantly different.

Each time I have written about 'sacking out', I have attempted to make it clear that I was referring to the process that my father used throughout the 1930s, 1940s and 1950s. It was for him the centrepiece of 'breaking' the horse. Today we often see it in the context of torturing prisoners of war to break them down.

My father would take an untrained, raw horse and tie him high to a substantial post in a fence line made of heavy planks, passing the rope through the chin piece on the halter and then tying a knot around the horse's neck. Ultimately the horse would be tied approximately 7 feet from the ground.

With the raw horse securely tethered, my father would then tie a large cotton rope around the neck of the horse just in front of the shoulders. He would then cause the horse to step over that rope with one hind leg, which would allow him to use the neck portion to hoist the hind leg off the ground. The horse was then standing on three legs and likely to fall if he made a quick move. Next my father would fix a canvas to a long rope and throw it at the horse, causing him to take fright. This would result in the horse falling virtually every time it was done.

This was the system my father called 'sacking out'. Injuries were commonplace. Teeth were knocked out as the horses hit the fence, and lifelong scars were evident around the rear pasterns where the rope had broken the skin. My father would repeat the process daily, alternating hind legs, until the horse was too frightened to run and would stand for the 'sacking out' in a state of quivering fear. I was the witness to the 'sacking out' process virtually every day of my childhood.

In England, the term 'sacking out' may be used or the process may be called 'swinging'. One critic of mine wrote an article for a magazine in England saying that I was wrong to criticize 'sacking out' and that every yearling should be 'swung'. He said that it assisted the horseman in truly breaking the horse so that it became subservient to the wishes of the handler.

'Swinging' is similar to what my father did except that it employs a free-standing single strong post about 10 feet high. The yearling is tied to that post right up near the top. No legs are tied up, but the process of frightening the horse with plastic or canvas is essentially the same procedure used by my father. With 'swinging', however, the frightened horse runs around the post, wrapping himself up like a tetherball. Once he has made sufficient circles of the post, then his rope is so short that he's actually lifted so that his front legs are off the ground.

It is this action that causes the process to be called 'swinging'.

I use many forms of frightening objects while training horses: pieces of plastic, canvas, cloth and other things. However, it is absolutely essential to my methods that the horses are allowed to move of their own free will. I use a Dually halter and encourage the horse to stay with me, but I do not restrain by tying. In every way I attempt to treat the horse in such a way as to cause as little elevation of adrenaline as possible.

Once I have the horse allowing the frightening object near it, then I am quick to retract the object when the horse settles even in the slightest. Through this method I enable the horse to rationalize that he is in control of the process of causing the object to go away. It is amazing how quickly this method will affect an acceptance of these scary things. True, it is an art form, and one must learn how far to go and when to back off. However, it is much more effective than what I regard as 'sacking out'.

My entire training programme is steeped in the premise that one should never force the horse, but always allow the horse a choice. I go so far as to say that it is not right to say 'you must' to the horse; instead, we must request him to do what we wish. The methods that I use and endorse will, in fact, cause the horse to accept frightening things in his life, not because he is forced to but eventually because he chooses to.

Recommended additional resources: 1, 5

Question 79

I have a horse that is one-sided. He is perfectly fine to handle on one side, but I can do nothing with him on the other. What do I do?

Answer

This one-sidedness can result from either of two opposite causes. It could be that the horse has been handled virtually entirely on the good side, ignoring the opposite side; or it could be that the horse has been abused on the bad side. No matter which is the case, the process to

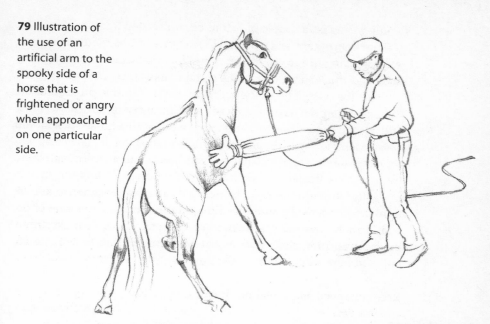

79 Illustration of the use of an artificial arm to the spooky side of a horse that is frightened or angry when approached on one particular side.

correct it is virtually the same. I suggest that you use Join-Up. I recommend three or four sessions on consecutive days or until your horse is relaxed, following you and perfectly comfortable being with you.

Having accomplished a good Join-Up or even two, I would add to that two or three sessions with the Dually halter. I would then begin to work on the bad side with an artificial arm. The artificial arm will allow you to work effectively with your adrenaline down. Gradually gain the trust of your horse, and this problem will go away.

I make an artificial arm often using a hard wood cane of the figure 7 shape. This means that there is almost no crook to the handle. I wrap it in sponge and tape the sponge in place. With the whole cane covered in sponge, a glove can be placed over the figure 7. You can stuff the glove with bits of cloth to fill it out and make it hand-like. The top of the 7 goes in the thumb, making the fingers soft and the thumb stiff. Having taped the glove in place, I recommend that one put a sleeve from an old sweatshirt or some such piece of clothing over the handle of the cane. Most canes are a bit short, so I extend them by tightly wiring on a couple of feet of discarded wooden rake handle.

This instrument will enable you to keep out of the danger zone while working to rub, scratch or even lift a hind leg using the figure 7 cane, allowing you to relax in the certain knowledge that you are safe.

Once the horse allows the artificial arm to rub him all around his bad side, then the handler can add to the degree of difficulty. A tiny little plastic bag will seem like a lethal weapon to a horse such as you have described. A good job of working with this small plastic bag will soon set your horse up so that you can have a half a dozen big plastic bags on the artificial arm and rub him generously with them.

All the time this work is being done, a good horseperson will be thinking of encouraging the horse to understand that this side of his body can be touched without force or pain. If his fear is simply inherent and not the result of harsh treatment, the system I have outlined here will be just as effective.

Recommended additional resources: 1, 13

Question 80

Monty – I have a twelve-month-old filly that is unhandled and may have had a traumatic experience when (along with her mother) she was caught at eight months to be weaned and purchased by us. She will eat from our hand, stand very, very close, but will not allow us to touch her. I have read everything I can get my hands on, but cannot find any advice on our next move. The filly has very, very overgrown feet, and we have to get hold of her for the farrier in the immediate future. There is quite an urgency regarding this problem.

Answer

Any person preparing a horse to be trimmed or shod by the farrier should take this responsibility seriously. I have seen extremely wild and fractious horses that require a week or more to be prepared for the farrier's visit. During this training period the sessions might take up to an hour a day. Half-hour sessions twice a day is not a bad idea.

In every country I have visited, I have found that some people believe that the farrier can educate the horse himself when it comes to standing and behaving while the footwork is done. This is an unacceptable expectation. A farrier is a professional and should be treated as such. His expertise is to care for your horse's feet, not to train him. While it is true that some farriers are also good horsemen and quite capable of doing the training, most horse owners do not plan to pay the farrier for training services.

The farrier often feels that he is being taken advantage of and should not be required to take the time necessary to train. This can result in short tempers, and horses being dealt with in an inappropriate way. While farriers are generally physically fit, muscular and capable of administering harsh treatment, should something like this occur, the blame should rest with the horse's owner, not the farrier.

Starting to prepare your horse to meet the farrier should preferably be done just after weaning, but you might inherit an older horse that has not had this education. What I'm outlining here is the following procedure for yearlings and older horses.

I would suggest that your student be introduced to the round pen and go through one, two or three Join-Ups on successive days. Once Join-Up has been achieved and your horse is perfectly willing to follow you with her adrenaline down and volunteers to stay with you comfortably, I suggest that you put her though two or three daily sessions with the Dually halter. If you don't feel safe working with your filly in this manner, bear in mind that there are plenty of educational opportunities to help you in this endeavour, as well as professional trainers who can support your efforts.

Once that has been accomplished, you are well on your way to having your horse stand comfortably while you pick up and deal with her feet. To begin the farrier-schooling process, you should first rub your horse over or spray her with insect repellent. She will find it disconcerting if she has to stand on three legs and can't stomp one to remove an insect.

After the repellent is applied, you can begin to pick each foot up repeatedly. If at this juncture your horse is perfectly willing to give you one foot at a time and stand on the other three while you tap on the lifted foot and run a rasp over it, you are probably ready to give your farrier a call. If your student is reluctant, offers to kick or refuses to allow you to tap or rasp the lifted foot, I suggest that you fabricate an 'artificial arm', as described in the answer to Question 79.

At this point, the good horseperson should reflect on why a horse might react in this fashion. Each of us should quickly remember that the flight animal relies upon his legs to carry him to safety when threatened by predators. We should immediately understand that acting violently towards the horse does nothing but convince him that we are predators and are out to cause him harm. Delivering pain to your student is absolutely inappropriate.

If your equine student wants to kick the artificial arm, do not discourage her; just return the arm to the position that bothered her until she accepts it anywhere you want to put it. Begin using the arm by massaging the body, shoulders and hips of the horse before proceeding to her legs. You can even rub the belly and up between the hind legs. Spend considerable time in the area of the flank, as it will often be touched by the farrier's shoulder. Bad habits can get started if the horse is still sensitive in the flank area before the leg-lifting procedures begin. Use the arm to massage all four legs until the horse is perfectly happy dealing with the procedure. Now you should have no trouble picking up each foot in turn and tapping it – at which point it is reasonable to ask your farrier to visit.

Recommended additional resources: 1, 7, 15

Question 81

Have you ever come across a horse so wild and dangerous that he was beyond help?

Answer

No. I have placed this question in this category hoping that the reader's mind will be jogged to realize that if mustangs are the wildest and most dangerous horses on earth and can still be helped, then any horse can be helped. I have worked with some mustangs that seemed, from how they behaved in their first lessons, to be absolutely lethal, and yet in a few days became relatively gentle.

Obviously, with the experience of hundreds of mustangs, it is easier for me to accomplish these improvements. But the principles remain the same for any horseperson: it is simply a matter of getting your work right, meeting the needs of your horse and carrying out the procedures that will accomplish the changes that you require to meet your goals.

MEDICAL AND PHYSICAL

The fact that I am not a practising equine veterinarian does not mean I allow myself to languish uneducated in the needs of our horses from a medical and physical perspective. Learning about and remaining aware of those needs is an essential part of becoming a successful horseperson. Nevertheless, whatever information I impart to the reader should be taken as coming from a layperson and not as a substitute for professional advice.

It is my opinion that every horseperson should take responsibility for seeking information about the discoveries that are constantly being made in healthcare for horses. Natural substances are constantly being developed to assist in healing wounds, averting diseases and recuperating from injury or sickness more effectively.

Personally, I find it a lot of fun to research state-of-the-art discoveries and then testing them so that I can assist others by recommending those that I feel are worth pursuing.

Question 82

I have a nine-year-old Missouri Fox Trotter that seems to stumble quite a bit while being ridden in the pasture or on a road, yet is very surefooted on trails. I read that having the cinch (girth) too tight could cause this. Is it possible he is bored and just not paying attention?

Answer

I don't think he is bored, and I don't believe the problem is a result of anything that was done to him in the past or that the cinch is too tight. I think you should take a hard look at the surfaces you are riding on and possibly have the veterinarian check for arthritic potential. Early arthritic changes often compromise the horse's range of motion. If surfaces are slightly uneven, this can easily cause stumbling.

If early arthritic changes are evident, it is possible to help your horse by amending how his feet are trimmed and shod. There are also many substances available today that will assist your horse in overcoming the problems of a compromised range of motion. Glucosamine and chondroitin, as well as glucosamine sulphate, are often suggested these days; also, many horsepeople use hyaluronic acid, which is available in both injectable and ingestible forms, as their treatment of choice for joint problems.

I have used all of the above with favourable results. However, I am not a veterinarian, and I would advise that you seek the opinion of a good equine practitioner, who will be able to tailor the treatment to your particular problem. I would not choose to speculate on the best course of action without seeing the horse and listening to the advice of a good veterinarian.

Question 83

I have a beautiful Thoroughbred mare that has a re-occurring melanoma situated high on the inner thigh. I have had it surgically removed twice, and it is currently returning. This particular growth is located squarely over a large blood vessel. The vets tell me that they would not like to attempt further surgeries. Any suggestions?

Answer

I have seen some dramatic results in cases such as this with the use of the supplement Transfer Factor™. Your situation sounds dire, and I suppose there are simply no guarantees in circumstances such as this. I have, however, seen massive lesions which have disappeared within six months of beginning systemic administration of Transfer Factor, which may be obtained through 4Life Research, 9580 S. 300 W., Sandy, Utah 84070; telephone 00 1 801 562 3600; www.4life.com.

Transfer Factor is a substance that I take myself. A company came to me in an attempt to get me to endorse it because of its value to horses. I inquired what it would do for people and was told that it was very effective in bolstering the horse and human immune system. I was further told that it would not be injurious to the human, and so I went on it myself. Later I used Transfer Factor to assist many horses in my care – the results have been dramatically positive in many instances.

I am pleased to inform you that I have now been taking Transfer

Factor for seven years. It seems that I have been exposed to the same level of viral and bacterial episodes that I always was. There has been one marked difference, however. I have not been sick with either a viral or a bacterial illness in these seven years. I am constantly around people on aeroplanes and in public places who are coughing or otherwise experiencing all the problems we humans go through. I might feel the tingle of a sore throat for two hours. I might have a slightly upset stomach and feel as though the flu is coming on, then wake up in the morning to feel just fine.

I am convinced that Transfer Factor, along with Co-enzymeQ10 (a natural substance, generally derived from fish, which increases the oxygen in the bloodstream), has made a remarkable difference in my ability to ward off viruses and bacteria. I would strongly suggest giving it a try with your horse.

Question 84

Do you have any advice for equine veterinarians to make their jobs safer and easier, besides using drugs/sedatives to control horses' behaviour?

Answer

As I travel the world, the question about veterinarians handling horses comes up regularly. I often speak at universities that run courses in veterinary science, and obviously I deal with equine veterinarians on a regular basis. As with farriers, the actions of these professionals have a substantial impact on the behaviour of horses.

Veterinary and farriery schools can only educate applicants from today's population. With that in mind we must realize that fewer and fewer of our young people are raised in a rural environment. While there are some top-notch young people coming into both professions, most of those seeking to learn these skills are city-reared youngsters. That being the case, all horse owners must realize that we have an obligation to assist these professionals, wherever we can, while they are working on the horses we are responsible for.

I recommend that horse owners pick the best professionals they can find and, whenever possible, plan to be present when they visit their horses. Young veterinarians and farriers spend less and less time during the course of their education with live horses. It is very difficult for schools to provide the time and the animals necessary to implement what I consider to be an appropriate allotment of 'hands-on' training.

Under these circumstances I feel it is imperative that horsepeople accept the responsibility for giving farriers and veterinarians the information they need to carry out their work in an acceptable manner. I often recommend that owners study my concepts with the serious intent of becoming proficient in working with their animals in the absence of violence; and I often further recommend that they loan to their professionals the materials they have used during the process of their education. Videos, DVDs, the weekly question-and-answer column posted on my website, my quarterly publication called the *Join-Up Journal*, my books, and the courses taught by Monty Roberts Certified Instructors worldwide are the primary sources of this information.

There is no value in confrontation with your horse or your professional. All your dealings with both should take place within an attitude of cooperation. There should be discussions about the intent to become more competent both as owners and as professional service providers. Many of our young professionals desire these opportunities rather than resist them. If your veterinarian or farrier is reluctant to accept a non-violent approach, change to another.

Recommended additional resources: 1, 3, 7, 9, 13, 14, 15, 16

Question 85

Would you say that it is acceptable to geld horses in order to make them easier to handle?

Answer

I firmly believe that only trained professionals should handle stallions. When I use the term 'trained professionals', I am referring to professional horsepeople who are very experienced in practical hands-on work with stallions. It is my opinion that all entire male horses that will potentially be handled by amateurs should be castrated.

I have many strong reasons for making this recommendation, far too many to list here. Above all, the danger factor is just too high. One cannot entirely control nature. I have witnessed too many injuries and deaths where amateurs and stallions were involved. Often I find it dangerous enough when professionals are handling stallions, and I am not comfortable advising casual horsepeople to expose themselves to these potential natural risks. Suffice it to say that stallions should be castrated unless they are going to be controlled throughout their lives by highly skilled individuals.

I have had some of my greatest successes in competition with geldings. Even though I have been a professional in the horse business virtually all of my life, I would now greatly prefer to ride and handle a gelding. They are effective in competition and, in my opinion, have lost none of their zest for life.

Recommended additional resource: 6

Question 86

What is your perspective on the natural diet of the horse?

Answer

While it is true that I have spent a lot of time with the mustangs, one must remember that these animals are native to the North African grasslands. About two thousand years ago, horses were grazing very much as the zebra grazes today.

The zebra, along with about a half a million wild horses, are free to graze over vast areas with a variety of plants that grow at different altitudes during the course of the four seasons. Soil and climatic disparity will also provide a menu far more variable than domestic horses are offered. These individuals are also privileged to graze in relative tranquillity. Generally they are able to see for great distances in every direction providing them with a safety factor important to good digestion. While predation can be a factor, wild horses are generally more psychologically healthy than the vast majority of the domestic ones. It is said that their diet was very rich in the grasses first of North Africa, then of Asia, the steppe countries and up into Russia.

I am told the American mustang discovered a veritable smorgasbord of plants – a wider variety than their predecessors found at their point of origin. I observed mustangs doing a great deal more pruning of bushes and trees than I had ever expected before my extended visits into their habitat. In addition, I discovered a greater tendency to migrate to higher and lower elevations as the seasons changed.

The grasses of the Great Basin area, including most of Nevada, northern New Mexico and Arizona, northern California, eastern Oregon and Idaho, and even reaching into Montana and Wyoming, contain many varieties of grama, rye, brome-grass and even a list of legumes. These plants made up approximately 80 per cent of the diet of the American mustang.

It is common to see mustangs grazing on a variety of small bushes and eating the lower leaves of various strains of poplar tree, and even the sycamore where they are available. In drought, one will often see mustangs clearing the leaves from groves of willows growing in low areas that supported the last of the standing water.

It is not uncommon to see these horses biting off, chewing and swallowing small limbs of trees, and it seems to me that this does no harm to their digestive tract or their overall health. It is also apparent to any close observer that mustangs spend a lot of time cleaning up seeds from dry desert floors, which to the casual glance would look barren and totally without nutritional material.

When one observes the overall health of these incredible animals, one must appreciate the value of this type of diet. The mustang's feet are vastly more healthy and strong than the feet of our domestic horses. While the environment itself has something to do with that, nutrition obviously plays a large role.

Clearly the majority of horse owners today are trying to meet the nutritional needs of their horses. I encourage the reader to stay updated on state-of-the-art findings where nutrition is concerned. I further encourage natural foot care and allowing horses to go unshod wherever possible.

Question 87

Do you have any thoughts about handlers or riders that are plus-sized?

Answer

For about the last thirty years of my life, I have been plus-sized! In my opinion, it is critical for the large rider to be very careful about the fit of their saddle and the quality of the padding under the saddle.

It is important for heavy people to understand that frequent rest periods are necessary if you are on a trail ride or extended session of any kind. About twenty minutes is as long as a rider of more than two hundred pounds ought to be on their horse's back without a break.

The type of horse one chooses is also important. The plus-sized rider would be well advised to spend their time on the backs of horses that are built suitably for heavyweights. A strong Quarter Horse or Warmblood with a short, muscular back is far better suited to handle the weight than, for instance, an Arab that might have a long, narrow back. However, it would be unfair to single out particular breeds with regard to suitability; while one must realize that some breeds are typically stronger and more capable of carrying heavyweights than others, it would be quite possible to find an Arab with a very short and extremely strong back.

Question 88

When you were studying horses in the wild, did you ever notice how many of them appeared lame? Was it at all possible to ascertain from where the lameness originated? And were any of the symptoms at all similar to lamenesses that can be detected in trained and ridden horses? Any thoughts on this subject would be very greatly valued.

Answer

I love this question, and it calls on me to search portions of my memory that have been neglected for decades. Lameness observed in the wild is substantially different in character from lameness observed in domestic ridden horses. Statistics will show that ridden horses will most often be lame from conditions affecting the front legs. These problems will be seen most often in the fetlock joint or the feet of the forelegs. The knees will also produce a fair percentage of lameness in the ridden horse.

What we are experiencing is pressure-induced damage through concussion and/or twisting motions. Racehorses, for instance, will express lameness on the forelimbs at a rate of approximately 85 per cent, while horses running in the wild will often tend to damage hooves while travelling over stones or rough ground. Obviously, no wild horse is protected by the shoes the domestic horse often wears while being ridden. Damage to feet incurred by wild horses is distributed about equally in fore and hind feet. I have seen the feet of wild horses actually split in half. The wild horse will also suffer from infections caused by bruising or open wounds, while injuries in the domestic horse will in most cases be medicated to counter the infection. Abrasions and punctures are far more plentiful on the limbs of horses running wild than they are on those of our domestic partners. The domestic horse will tend to suffer far more from injuries of a concussive nature than from those caused by sharp objects.

In studying wild horses, one should also bear in mind that in many cases they are the survivors and therefore the fittest: wild horses with fragile, thin-walled feet would die young and not reproduce those shortcomings. When I look at the bottom of a wild horse's foot, it is obvious at once that there are significant differences when compared with domestic feet. The walls are thicker, the angle of the foot is steeper and the sole is akin to the hide of a rhino.

Some of these characteristics are the result of constant work without protective covering. Young kids in poor countries who run around barefooted can walk over broken glass without a grimace.

Most of us who wear good shoes can hardly get around when barefooted. Similarly, if our domestic horses were just turned loose barefooted to survive in the wild, most of them would have a very difficult time until their feet hardened up to stand the rigours of that environment.

In conclusion, let me say that lameness is substantially different in domestic and in wild horses. I might add that I published an article in issue 1 of the 2003 *Join-Up Journal* called 'The Advantage of Going Bare', which outlines the power of riding barefoot horses to improve the quality of the hoof structure. The article is reproduced on my website, www.montyroberts.com.

Recommended additional resource: 16

Question 89

Herbal remedies are a controversial issue. I have been doing some research about them and was wondering what you thought about these remedies, such as lavender oil, Bach flower remedies, Rescue Remedy, etc. Do they really work or will they hurt my horse?

Answer

I have no evidence that herbal remedies have ever hurt a horse. I use Rescue Remedy for myself and I have used Rescue Remedy for horses, too. I also use Rescue Cream and an assortment of Bach flower remedies. It is very difficult to prove that they are effective, but I feel certain that they are doing no harm. The evidence in favour of Rescue Remedy is quite strong, and I know that many people worldwide are using it for many purposes. However, one should never allow the use of herbal remedies to exclude the potential for conventional care and medication. An experienced equine veterinarian should consistently be consulted so as to give one's horse the best of both worlds.

I am a strong believer in Transfer Factor™. There is an enormous bank of evidence being logged as we speak about how effective this natural substance is in bolstering the immune system. I have some very strong evidence of how effective it is.

My wife, Pat, is active in helping me study many of these natural substances, such as CoQ10 and grape seed extract (oligomeric proanthocyanidins). I can say with strong conviction that many of these natural substances work, and I do not know of any that would hurt your horse. As for their being controversial, this would imply that there's a potential for harm, and I don't believe that is a reasonable assumption. The only part of all of this that might be controversial is whether or not you would choose to spend the money on them. I do, and that is my choice. No controversy here.

Question 90

A lot of people in dressage believe in the need for stretching exercises for their horses in order to improve the collection of the horse. Does the Western performance horse need this?

Answer

If dressage horses need pre-session stretching to the extent of an 8 out of a perfect 10, then Western horses need pre-session stretching at a 9.9 out of a perfect 10. It is my belief that a flexible and well-aligned cutting or reining horse is far better prepared to give you a top performance than one without those advantages.

The Western horses here at Flag Is Up Farms go through an extensive daily stretching regime. Phillip Ralls, who trains our Western horses, is a qualified equine physiotherapist and, like his father Ron Ralls, has been a leader in this practice.

Too many of us tend to allow our minds to travel differently if we think 'flat saddle' or 'Western'. Our horses have little idea what style saddle goes on their backs, and their physiological needs are just as important no matter what the discipline.

In our operation, I recommend the use of food to induce horses to execute the stretching procedures appropriate. I do not, however, recommend offering these tidbits from the human hand. Bits of carrot provide a palatable inducement. It is my recommendation that the horseman place the piece of carrot on a small hook that is fixed to the end of a stick about 3 feet (1 metre) long.

Very little time is required to educate the horse to the point where he can reach some weird places so as to pull a small bit of carrot from its hook. My horse Nic will crane his neck all the way to an area near either of his stifles for a bit of carrot. He will also drop his head and place it between his knees reaching nearly halfway to his hocks in order to get his treat.

Stretching the show jumper, the dressage horse and the Western horse is likely to prevent injuries and at the same time produce an anatomy that is more flexible. Obviously the flexible anatomy is far more capable of athletic performance than the non-flexible one.

Question 91

Do you have any advice for dealing with a horse that has impaired vision?

Answer

Unfortunately, no professional trainer can legally give advice on dealing with a sight-impaired horse, because if we were ever asked the question whether we had put you in the safest possible situation, we would have to answer no. Without working with the horse ourselves, we can only ask you to get professional help with your horse and make sure you always place both yourself and your horse in a safe environment. Flight animals are dependent on their vision for many reasons, and your horse will have adapted its behaviour to compensate for this lost sense.

Good luck and please remember to make sure you and your horse stay safe and enjoy working together!

FOALS AND FOAL IMPRINTING

This is a relatively new science brought to us by Dr Robert Miller, who has become a good friend as well as a study partner in my journey to becoming a better horseman. Foal imprinting has been going on for millions of years. It's just that we humans have taken a long time to catch on.

When I say that foal imprinting has been going on for millions of years, I am simply referring to the fact that newborn horses log into their brains their early experiences. At the time of birth there is a window wide open to receive information and store it. This phenomenon is not exclusive to horses; it occurs in virtually every species that I have worked with, including humans.

In the 1950s, most child psychologists came to agree that placing the newborn human infant on the abdomen of the mother was a distinct aid in the bonding process. It is my opinion that imprinting the child can go much further. Bathing together and oil-assisted massages can be extremely helpful in the process of a child coming to accept important adults in their life.

Dr Miller has stayed with me on Flag Is Up Farms, and we have imprinted many foals together. I believe there are still many things to learn about this science, but there is no question in my mind that it offers a great deal in the area of causing equines to accept human beings into their life.

Question 92

What is 'foal imprinting'?

Answer

Imprinting is the act of introducing a young horse to the human at the time of birth. There is a window of opportunity at this time, which is open fully for only about an hour after the foal is born. This is the optimal time for imprinting. This is not to say that you cannot imprint after that hour, but it is not as effective. You should maintain good husbandry practices recommended for foaling, and imprinting should commence only when you are entirely comfortable that the foal is being born under normal circumstances, and that your actions are not interfering in any way with the mare's bonding with the foal.

While I have been a student of Dr Miller's foal-imprinting methods, I have allowed my experiences to modify the process. The 'imprinter' should place himself on his knees at the dorsal (back) side of the foal, near the withers. He should take care when handling the foal never to get between the mare and foal. There are many books and articles describing the procedure and timelines for foal imprinting. These include a book by Dr Miller titled *Imprint Training of the Newborn Foal: A Swift, Effective Method for Permanently Shaping a Horse's Lifetime Behaviour*, and my own textbook, which has a large section on this important topic.

Recommended additional resource: 1

Question 93

What is the most important thing I should know about dealing with a two-month-old foal?

Answer

The most important knowledge that I can impart to you is to be safe and work with your foal without violence or force. At two months of age, probably the most important work is leading the foal alongside his mother. I further suggest that it is important to groom and pick up feet, encouraging your foal to stand and to be comfortable with you during these procedures.

While foal imprinting is usually executed in the first hour of life, imprinting first impressions can be done right through the growing-up years. I would suggest studying the section on foal imprinting in my textbook, and also recommend books by Dr Robert Miller regarding the care and training of foals. One of the pitfalls I would suggest you take great care to avoid is feeding from the hand. It is also extremely important to understand the principles behind allowing a horse to remain a horse. Many people are guilty of over-humanizing the young horse.

Recommended additional resource: 1

Question 94

I have a six-month-old colt. Should I be doing Join-Up with him yet?

Answer

The process of establishing a relationship with your foal through Join-Up should begin once your foal has been successfully weaned and no longer calls out for his mother. Done properly, Join-Up will create a lifelong understanding between weanling and human. One or two Join-Up sessions should be enough to develop a trust-based relationship.

Keep in mind that too many sessions will be counterproductive – your foal will have the short concentration span typical of babies of all species, so any work done needs to reflect this. After completing Join-Up, you can develop your foal's skills at leading, being handled all over and having his feet picked up. I recommend that at this age your foal have a natural life, spending lots of time at pasture with other horses.

If you follow these guidelines you should have a happy, well-adjusted individual ready to begin his life with humans. A couple of Join-Ups at weaning time should be very helpful and allow you to get through the growing-up phase of your horse in good order. Should you experience difficulties between, let's say, eight months and twenty-four months, a couple more Join-Ups might be beneficial. Schooling to the Dually halter can also make life a lot easier for both you and your young horse.

Recommended additional resources: 1, 3, 5

Question 95

Do you have any advice about orphans? We had a wonderful mare
that died a few days ago and want to make sure we are doing the
right things with the surviving foal.

Answer

Orphans present the horseperson with a challenge and a huge responsibility. If we are going to raise an orphan to become a useful and cooperative adult, then several factors must be addressed and acted upon. Our first responsibility is to keep the foal alive and healthy. Contact your veterinarian for suggestions on how best to do this.

Check your local area to see if anyone has a bank of colostrum, which is the first milk the mare produces after giving birth to a foal. It is important to bolster the immune system of the newborn by providing this vital nourishment. You could also inquire as to the availability of nurse mares in your community.

If you can arrange for this foal to be raised by a foster mother, it is far more likely that it will grow up to be a normal adult horse. If no nurse mare is available, remember that the red-letter rule is: *wherever possible, cause the foal to take nourishment without it being connected to the human hand.* I have raised foals quite successfully using goats. The female goat jumps up on a stand, puts its head in a neck yoke and eats a bit of grain while its foster foal nurses. Goat's milk is far better than cow's milk for raising foals. During the three months I have the foal nurse a goat, I will keep the foal with other mares and foals, if at all possible. There is a danger here, because the foal will try to nurse other mares. If there is an aggressive mare in the field, one should remove her and her foal for safety's sake.

The foals should nurse about ten times each twenty-four hours during the first two to three weeks; by the time it is three months old it should be nursing only four to five times in each twenty-four-hour period. Throughout this span of time, one should be preparing the foal by introducing artificial feeds recommended by your veterinarian. There are many artificial preparations for feeding foals today, and most do a pretty good job. Remember to investigate ways to deliver these preparations to the foal without involving a human. At the end of three months, the foal can go on with dry supplemental feeding quite nicely, but should remain in the presence of other foals, if at all possible.

If one is successful at finding a foster nurse mare, then the goat and artificial feeds are unnecessary.

Each of the measures that I have recommended here has been successful for me with the many foals Pat and I have raised.

Throughout the rearing of an orphan foal, one should take care to handle and interact with the foal as normally as you possibly can. Try in every way not to treat the foal as something special or particularly lovable. Orphan foals often turn out to be quite aggressive and mean because they become too humanized.

EXTRA-OLD HORSES

At age seventy-two, I have outlived many wonderful horses. Dealing with them in the autumn of their lives was seldom easy, but provided me with many hours of reflection on more active times. I can remember clearly conversations I had with Brownie and Johnny Tivio about the good old days.

We humans have domesticated the horse. We have created a world for horses far different from the natural environment they lived in for about fifty million years. We have built fences to confine their movement and essentially removed almost all of the predators that moulded their survival-of-the-fittest mentality.

There are probably fewer than half a million wild horses remaining on earth, while at one time there were probably more than twenty million. These remaining herds live in a few isolated areas, and fewer than a hundred thousand of them are subject to serious predation. This means that we have horses living a great deal longer than they did before domestication.

'Stewardship' is a word that comes to mind to convey what I believe is our responsibility to the horse under current conditions. We are obliged to assist in any way possible to cause our elderly horses to have a reasonable quality of life. The fact that horses have a lifespan considerably shorter than we humans dictates that we will experience life's end for many of our equine partners. Dealing with that fact is one of the most important responsibilities that any horseperson has.

As it turns out, many of the horses that I have known and loved have died of natural causes. Brownie, Night Mist and Johnny Tivio head the list in this category. At the same time, Julia's Doll, Quincy Feature and Pepinics Dually each reached a point where pain and the inability to move about comfortably reduced their quality of life to what I consider to be unacceptable. At that point, a veterinarian injected them and they went to sleep painlessly; they all have gravestones on Flag Is Up Farms.

Each of us is obligated to decide for ourselves what is a reasonable solution to the question of stewardship. So long as you love the horse and are considering its best interest, I have confidence you will reach the appropriate decision.

Question 96

I have a thirty-six-year-old stallion and for three years I have had a problem with him. Every time I walk my horse with a halter only to a venue to work with him, he just stands still on the road or in front of the door. I have the feeling he does not respect me. When my teacher, who has helped me learn to ride the horse, walks behind the two of us, he just walks in the indoor school hall right away. But if my friend does the same and urges him to move, my horse only makes one step.

He does not only threaten to kick people, he does it! My friend has had an accident with this horse already. Could you please help?

Answer

At thirty-six years of age, this horse is by most accepted standards well into his nineties in human terms. No matter how difficult 'Great-grandfather' seems to be, the family generally doesn't discuss ways to re-train him. There comes a time for every person and every horse when responsibilities are a thing of the past, and retirement is well earned in our nineties. I would do this old horse no favour if I started discussing ways to improve his behaviour.

Green grass, fresh water and a loving person to groom and care for him is what this old fellow needs at this time, and all I would recommend for him. When you have a similar problem with a horse of an age more reasonable for training then you will find me recommending my Dually halter.

Recommended additional resource: 5

Question 97

I have an eighteen-year old gelding that has been a wonderful horse for me. He seems healthy and relatively sound, but is a bit arthritic and beginning to stumble a little. Is there any way I can help him through these senior years giving him a bit more quality time?

Answer

It seems to me that you are involved in this quality time as well. This is not a bad thing, as you have obviously had many years with this senior citizen, which were probably fun for him too. I am not one to believe that horses wish to be inactive. It is my opinion that they prefer to have enjoyable activities for as long as possible.

You are the only one who can judge when the horse is in pain during your rides and when he is enjoying it. Thanks to modern discoveries, there are many safe ways to keep a horse from suffering joint pain in his senior years. Arthritic joints are responsible for most of the pain that older horses feel when ridden.

I must immediately stress here that I am not a practising equine veterinarian, and that I recommend consulting an appropriate equine practitioner where any medical problem exists. Nevertheless, horsepeople should keep themselves aware of substances and procedures that will assist in keeping horses healthy. The better informed you are of the horse's physiology, the better chance you have promptly to address the needs of the horse. Please read my advice as that of a layperson, and then check with an equine practitioner before acting upon any recommendation that I make.

Knees, fetlocks, hocks and feet that have accumulated wear and tear from years of activity can be safely assisted with preparations that have been recently discovered. Glucosamine is the first substance that I will discuss. I have used it successfully on horses and on myself. I tend to feel better about medicating my horse only after I know the substance I am giving him is relatively safe for people too.

Chondroitin is a substance used most often in conjunction with glucosamine. I have taken this preparation for the past five years or so with no ill effects and some rather astonishing positive results. It is designed to help by strengthening the cartilaginous tissue of the joints, and most equine practitioners feel that it is beneficial.

Recently, I have been testing the ingestible form of hyaluronic acid. About a tablespoonful each evening has been on my regime for the past ninety days, and I must say that my back and my old worn-out knees are unquestionably slightly more comfortable than they were before I began taking it. I don't believe very many humans are using it yet, but I believe this will change in the future.

There are other substances, too; but one should remember that a good diet and regular exercise are essential for horses, just as they are for people. Keeping down the carbohydrates so as to reduce heat and energy build-up in your horse is a good idea. Watching the horse's weight has a lot to do with how comfortably his joints function.

Put all of these recommendations together with a visit from a good veterinarian, mix them up and then sit down in the stable with your horse and consider what is best for him. It is your responsibility to make a decision that is in the best interests of both yourself and your horse. Thank you for asking the question; the final answer is really in your hands.

ENTRY LEVEL: BEGINNERS AND BUYING YOUR FIRST HORSE

Obviously, this is one of the most important sections to anyone with that wild expectation of finally getting their first horse. So many wide-eyed youngsters approach me with questions during this time of anticipation; we professionals in the horse world owe new entrants our greatest effort to assist them. Anything we can do to reduce the number of mistakes they make is good for the horse industry.

It is the professional's obligation to advise the prospective new owner on the importance of staying safe. Safety should be the first priority, as accidents and injuries can all too easily detract from the enjoyment of being with horses.

Protecting a future owner from unscrupulous profit seekers is also a very important factor. We in the horse industry have among us far too many incompetent people with the gift of the gab and an intent to deceive for profit. Fortunately, we also have among us many knowledgeable people who are fair and properly educated and motivated to assist new and experienced owners. It is the obligation of each of us who would call ourselves a professional to guide newcomers in the right direction.

Question 98

I rode and owned ponies as a child, but gave up in my teens to study and socialize. I'd like to take up riding again at sixty-seven, but I am so very nervous when riding. I've been told that Icelandic horses have a wonderful disposition for the senior rider. I would be grateful for any advice you are able to give me, as I enjoy horses so much and want a positive experience.

Answer

I think every breed has individuals that fall into the category of being safe and 'bomb proof'. Having said that, every breed also has its share of challenging individuals that might be less than safe and reliable.

The Icelandic horses that I have worked with certainly have had the capacity to become gentle, steady and sensible. The gait of the Icelandic is fine for a beginning rider. They are smooth and comfortable when properly trained.

I have now worked with probably something over five hundred Icelandic horses. On this basis of experience I feel qualified to express the opinion that, with proper schooling, the Icelandic can become a very good choice for a horseperson in their senior years.

The gait of the Icelandic is called the 'tolt', and is similar to that of several other breeds: the Tennessee Walking Horse, the Missouri Fox Trotter, the Rocky Mountain Horse and, of course, the Peruvian Paso and the Paso Fino, to name a few. Without personal experience, I have it from reliable sources that the tolt and other gaits of this kind offer a ride that is smooth, comfortable and level with the ground. It is said that you can take a glass of wine with you and never spill a drop. These folks go on to tell me that the tolt is much less likely to cause a rider to be muscle sore from the experience.

The most important piece of advice that I can give you is that whatever horse you choose should be a safe individual no matter what breed it is. Colour, breed or other aesthetic virtues should be way down lower on your list of priorities than safety. The second consideration should be health and soundness, and then we go on through a list of about twenty important aspects in selecting an appropriate horse. It is crucial that you get this decision right, as it will affect your relationship with the horse and your own safety and enjoyment for a long period of time.

Recommended additional resource: 11

Question 99

What should I look for when buying a horse for the first time?

Answer

This project has many facets, and most of them are critically important if you are to have a positive experience. I go into all these matters in great detail in the educational resources listed in the

'Recommended Additional Resources' section at the back of this book, so here will just mention a few of the factors you will need to consider. I take into consideration the financial aspects, not just of buying the horse but also of keeping it, as well as the kind of horse one might want and matching the horse to one's own level of skill and experience.

Safety is a factor that I stress throughout any advice I give on purchasing a horse. After safety comes health and soundness, the time needed to devote to the horse and whether or not that time is available. Stabling and who will care for the horse are important. I even go into waste disposal – something that most people forget.

In the process of selecting a horse, it is critical to engage the assistance of a veterinarian who specializes in your chosen field. A professional horseperson of long-standing good character can be very helpful in keeping one from buying the wrong horse. I even recommend a farrier be called in for a quick assessment of the feet and what will be required to keep them right.

Please do not simply accept these few important tips as sufficient guidance to prepare you for the purchase of a horse. I have gone into the whole subject in far greater detail in other published work, and it is critically important that you give the project proper consideration before you go ahead. Failing to do a good job of preparing yourself for the purchase of a horse will almost certainly result in a less than perfect outcome.

Recommended additional resource: 11

Question 100

Do you think it is beneficial to ride bareback?

Answer

The better riders we are, the better chance our horses have to perform the tasks we request. Riding bareback is one very good way to learn to be a better rider. I rode bareback extensively as a child and feel that it was helpful in training me to be constantly aware of the position of my horse's body and his movements as he negotiated turns, lead changes and stops.

I am a firm believer that if we are to be good riders we should learn to ride both bareback and with a saddle. I further believe that we should at least know the basic principles for the correct riding in as many styles of saddle as possible: Western, English hunt seat, dressage, park seat, Australian stock saddle, even Argentinean gaucho saddle. Knowledge is something none of us can have enough of; I even recommend that young riders should use a bareback pad at some stage in their education, as it is quite helpful for leg position.

Recommended additional resource: 16

Question 101

Why do we mount on the left side? Is it merely tradition or to do with the horse's physiology?

Answer

The fact that we mount on the left dates back in history to a time when horses were ridden primarily to go to war. Soldiers were equipped with sabres, routinely attached to the left leg. The right-handed trooper would draw his sabre across his body with the right hand. If you attempted to mount on the right side, you would have to use your right foot in the stirrup. This meant that your left leg was obliged to swing over the horse's back. With a sabre on that side, this would be very awkward and dangerous.

The officers trained young recruits to get on their horses with their sabre, rifle and backpack. This required a uniform set of regulations and, since most of the troops were right-handed, the left side of the horse was chosen for mounting. Thus it became known as the near side, and the other side as the off side.

Through the centuries it became the habit of all people who worked with horses to work from the left side. Most people working with driving horses would work from the near side because the harness was geared to be buckled from the near side; the bridle and headstall were also geared to buckle from the near side. Horses are habitually worked with from birth from the near side, so most horses respond better from that side.

FRUIT SALAD

This short section deals with a relatively new phenomenon in the horse industry. For centuries, there was very little in the way of educational opportunities for young horsepeople. Today, we are approaching overload in the range of available ways for people to become better educated in the ways of *Equus*.

Obviously this is a good problem, because over-education is better than under-education; but so great a range of possibilities has disadvantages as well as advantages Fortunately, the advantages outweigh the disadvantages; nevertheless, we should take a hard look at the negative side of this situation so that we are better prepared to take the course that will do most to improve the lives of our horses.

Concepts are coming to us from every direction, and while most are well intended, they differ from one another to degrees varying from slight to massive. The plethora of approaches and ideas becomes like a fruit salad, from which people often pick and choose among the vast array of concepts available. This mixture of ideas can often become quite confusing for our horses. It is essential that we become aware of this aspect of our current educational opportunities.

Question 102

I am currently doing Parelli Natural Horsemanship; I am a Level 1 Partnership student, going on to Level 2 Harmony. Is it OK to use more than one training method on a horse, like a mixture of Join-Up with Follow-Up and Parelli? Or should I just stick with one? Or should I do one training method on one horse, and another on a different one?

Answer

It is wonderful to hear that you are learning about different methods to communicate with your horse and enhance your partnership. In my opinion, you should continue to research all the available methods of horsemanship in order to make an informed decision on the most appropriate method for you and your horse. However, it is my recommendation that, in experimenting with different methods, you need to take great care not to confuse the horse.

There are many entry-level horsepeople in the world today. A high percentage of them are putting a lot of effort into becoming educated in working with horses. However, some of them are going about it as if the educational material available were like a fruit salad, picking out, say, the pineapple, the apricots and the cherries, passing over the nectarines and the pears. When this method is applied to a single horse, it is confusing.

My suggestion is to work with different horses, and use only one method on each horse. You can then observe their learning and come to a conclusion yourself as to the method with which you prefer to work. I believe that if you take this approach you will be more effective as a trainer and have much happier horses as well. I hope this helps and keep up the good work.

MINIS

I've had minimal experience with minis, but I believe that the good horseperson will take the attitude that miniature horses are still horses: that is, they may be in a smaller package, but their nature is extremely similar to that of their larger brothers and sisters.

It has always been my opinion that horses are horses, no matter the breed or the size. When we humans decided to manipulate genetics to produce miniature horses, we changed their anatomy, but not their psychological makeup. They are horses, and they possess all of the inherent behavioural tendencies of their species. We should not accept the temptation to regard them as cute little household pets. Their overall pattern of life is based on the natural tendencies of *Equus*.

Question 103

What are your views on the suitability of miniature horses for guiding the blind?

Answer

I must emphasize that I am not a therapist in this area. Please understand that I do not work with guide dogs. I sit as an interested observer. I have worked with seizure alert dogs and found them to be incredibly effective. While I have incorporated miniature horses in some of my corporate events and observed them being used as assistance animals, I am not fully aware of their value in guiding the blind. I am in favour of using horses as therapy animals wherever we can and for many purposes. I recommend that you use the Internet to seek out doctors and other therapists who are fully educated in the area of guide horses for the blind and consult them for their views.

Question 104

Are miniature horses appropriate for children as pets? I have read that they can be housebroken and actually live inside with the family. What are your thoughts?

Answer

I love horses, and for me I want them to remain horses. I don't think they should replace dogs or cats as house pets. I am all for horses, and any time they can bring light into the life of a child or indeed a person of any age, I am in favour of it. I happen to believe that, while dogs and cats make good pets, horses, being flight animals, make wonderful partners but should not be considered as pets.

I have not been closely associated with the world of miniature horses, and I don't want to purport to be an expert in this field. I do believe that minis are still horses, and they crave space in the outdoors even more than dogs and cats. All the inherent tendencies of the mini are quite close to those of normal-sized horses.

These factors lead me to believe that minis should be viewed as horses that are small, and not as pets. They can be trained to pull vehicles and most of the activities that horses take part in with the exception of carrying heavy weights. I am not opposed to minis learning to do tricks and entertaining the family in the ways of *Equus*.

DONKEYS AND MULES

I love mules. It is my opinion that on balance they are smarter than horses. I believe that the best thing about a donkey is that it's the only way to get a mule – and so I guess I love donkeys too, because they provide us with what is probably the most intelligent equine animal on earth.

Tina was a mule that I owned in the 1970s (she will feature in the answer in this section). I regard Tina as the most intelligent equine animal that I ever worked with. On at least one day, she was far more intelligent than me.

Scientists will agree that mules are true hybrids. The mule cannot reproduce. All true hybrids, zoological or botanical, barely ever reproduce. There is a term in genetics, 'hybrid vigour', that has to do with the fact that a male and female have come together to produce an offspring from extremely diverse genetic origins. When this occurs, the offspring tends to be bigger, stronger and more vigorous than those produced by genetically similar parents.

Question 105

Have you had any success with donkeys or mules?

Answer

Donkeys are a challenge. They are lovable creatures, and I have nothing against them. They're a little hard to train through the language because they have a less strongly developed flight mechanism than horses and are often not as responsive. Mules are wonderful. They respond beautifully to the training concepts I use. I have had many outstanding mules that became exemplary partners for packing, trail riding, roping, racing and reining. Mules have a long list of attributes and should not be taken lightly when it comes to performing in many disciplines.

Dr Robert Miller, the father of foal imprinting and long-time 'mule man', believes that Join-Up is the most effective way to train a mule. He has often told me that mules waited thousands of years for my message to come along. We have talked together many times about the widespread opinion that mules are stubborn. Dr Miller and I agree that most people fail to understand that the mule's level of intelligence is significantly higher than the horse's and that its seemingly stubborn streaks are expressions of intelligence. Mules will respond to harsh treatment with a staunch refusal to comply.

Virtually every horseperson has often heard old-timers say that the only way you can train a mule is to hit him on the head with a two-by-four to first get his attention. Clearly this is a statement based in abject ignorance. It still baffles me how we could go on for centuries failing to understand that horses and mules do a lot better in the absence of violence than in the presence of it.

The very behaviour of flight animals cries out to us, advising against the use of violence. I realize that men can become frustrated and resort to violence when they can't seem to think of anything else to do. The perplexing fact is how this mentality could dominate mainstream training techniques for centuries. If the reader of this book gets nothing out of it except an understanding of the principle of non-violence, I will consider it a great success.

When I work with mules, I often feel as though they are the teachers and I am the student. A good horseperson who trains mules and carefully observes their responses will ultimately become a better horseperson. Virtually every aspect of my work is more effective with mules than it is with horses. From Join-Up to my Dually halter, they are psychologically wired for the acceptance of my principles.

In my training operation I have worked with many mules. I had some of the best racing mules in competition, and I owned the World Champion Western Reining Mule for many years. Her name was Tina, and I wrote about her in my third book, where I told a story of how she outsmarted me on a cattle drive. She was great for gathering cattle and working in the branding pen.

Recommended additional resource: 2

DOGS

For me, horses are man's best friend, but I guess for most people that accolade goes to dogs. I hardly ever go through a question-and-answer session without a few questions about dogs. They are great, and I love working with dogs. However, I don't like to step on the territory of professional dog trainers when my experience bank is definitely with horses. I answer as best I can and direct my questioners towards those people who are far better qualified to deal with this species than I am.

Question 106

How do you feel your methods have impacted the dog-training world?

Answer

Although dogs and horses are essentially at opposite ends of the biological spectrum as predators and prey animals, there are significant similarities in the way you train behaviour in both species and, in fact, all species including humans.

There is a wonderful lady by the name of Jan Fennell who has developed a canine training methodology based on my concepts. She lives in England and has written, among others, a book called *The Dog Listener*, which I highly recommend. The ideals are of learning the animal's natural language and of training using trust and positive reinforcement work, regardless of the species. You can access Jan's website at www.janfennellthedoglistener.co.uk.

It is quite true that my discoveries have impacted the dog-training world and fortunately in a very positive way. Most professional dog trainers are using far less harsh measures than they were even ten years ago. You can see a strong movement to a more logical approach to training dogs through communication in recent years.

GAITED HORSES

Those training horses with special gaits are in a segment of the horse industry that will be most dramatically affected by the current revolution in training techniques. It is wrong to blame people for doing something if it is the only way they learned to do it. I feel that it is much better to give them new ideas rather than to blame them for the use of traditional ones.

The European area, including the UK, has seen huge growth in numbers of the gaited horses of Spain and Portugal. Icelandic horses, with their four and even five gaits, have arrived in Great Britain en masse. There are more than three hundred thousand Icelandic gaited horses in Germany alone. The Tennessee Walking Horse has established itself worldwide, along with the Missouri Fox Trotter and the Rocky Mountain Horse.

Competitions involving gaited horses have historically been judged on a system which awards more points to the competitors with the highest leg action. With that as the primary feature, many un-scrupulous people have trained these wonderful horses using brutal and often injurious techniques.

It is my position that none of these horses has done anything wrong. It is the people who have broken the rules of reasonable treatment. I have been criticized in the past for extolling the virtues of gaited horses, by people who believe that if there is inhumane activity then the breed itself should be punished. Obviously it is not the horses that are at fault, and I believe that every professional should encourage the breed associations to create stringent rules and enforce them to the letter. No gaited horse should be treated badly first by its owner and then once again by an uninformed public.

Question 107

I ride saddle seat and would like to use action chains. What do you think of them?

Answer

In recent years laws have been put in place to protect horses from pieces of equipment that cause pain. Under the US Horse Protection Act of 1970 action chains may be used within strict guidelines. The Regulations prescribe the enforcement of the Act, and the current 'Operating Plan' is an agreement between the US Department of Agriculture and the Tennessee Walking Horse industry regarding specific implementation of the Regulations. The USDA has set the pace for regulations governing the Tennessee Walking Horse world-wide, including the UK.

The action chains permitted under these regulations may be no heavier than 6 ounces (170 grams). This is the same weight as a Rolex Oyster Day/Date watch. I personally see no reason to classify this as a painful device. It is more like a bracelet. In disciplines where it is desirable to achieve foot elevation, the use of an action chain will encourage the horse to raise the foot higher than it would without the 'bracelet'. If it is used in a humane fashion, I can certainly accept it.

Question 108

I am interested in becoming more involved with horses of special gaits. I would like to hear your feelings on Icelandic horses, Peruvian Pasos, Paso Finos and the Tennessee Walking Horse.

Answer

It is obvious there is a special place for gaited horses within our industry. I find Icelandic horses to be quite remarkable in many ways. They are probably the purest breed we have on earth. For hundreds of years importation of horses to Iceland has been against the law. If an Icelandic horse leaves that country for any reason, it may not return to Iceland. There are no horses of any breed coming into Iceland. This has ensured a purity of these wonderful horses that virtually no other breed in the world enjoys. They are strong, durable and easy for the occasional rider to get along with.

The tolt (their special gait) is smooth, fast and easy to ride: no one gets saddle sores, even someone who rides very seldom. The disposition of the Icelandic horse is outstanding, and their physical attributes place them at the top of the list of tough horses that can do fine in harsh conditions.

The Peruvian Paso and the Paso Fino are close enough for me to comment on them together. They are the descendants of the Spanish Barb horses and others of North African blood. Like the Icelandic, these are small horses with big hearts and a wonderful, fast, tolt-like gait, which is said to be the smoothest available. These horses were bred to carry riders through the coffee plantations of South America and to go for miles and miles without tiring their riders.

The Tennessee Walking Horse is larger than any of the three breeds I have just described. They are strong and able to carry large riders for long distances. The Tennessee Walking Horse was bred to carry the cotton plantation owners of the Deep South in the United States.

Bred from English and North African bloodlines, the Walking Horse was chosen for its tendency to execute an even, 'single-footed' walk of four beats that carries the rider over the ground smoothly and rapidly. Its disposition is fantastic, and many experts consider it a breed suitable for a family, including small children and beginner riders.

The Tennessee Walking Horse has often been the centre of controversy regarding techniques used to win competitions. It has become fashionable to value most highly the horse that elevates the forefeet extremely high with each stride. To achieve this height of action, some people have apparently used techniques that are less than comfortable for the horse.

Recent laws have been enacted to discourage these procedures, and I am now active in assisting this breed in its effort to regain its deserved popularity worldwide. Not one Tennessee Walking Horse has ever done anything to deliberately cause pain to a human. We should not, then, condemn the breed, but only those who would use illegal techniques to enhance performance.

The breed itself has a long list of fantastic attributes, and in my opinion ought to be the breed of choice for many people in various parts of the world. The Tennessee Walking Horse is, for example, wonderful for trail riding through Bavaria or Austria and even Switzerland, and could be enjoyed in many other European countries.

Australia is a country made for the Tennessee Walking Horse. It is vast, and people there are found to be riding great distances. These horses will cover many miles a day, cause far less soreness to the rider than the mainstream breeds, and be safe for all ages and skill levels.

The United States is where the Tennessee Walking Horse was created, and yet here, because of a few cheaters, it has often been viewed askance by the public. This is extremely unfair to a wonderful group of horses ready to provide much enjoyment to US families who wish to ride.

The Tennessee Walking Horse travels with all three normal gaits in place; while it prefers the 'running walk' to the trot, one can canter the Tennessee Walking Horse, unlike some of the tolt breeds that find the canter undesirable. The Tennessee Walking Horse will be at home when ridden with any saddle made in the world.

Question 109

I was recently looking for a horse to buy. I wanted a gaited horse, so I visited a stable that specialized in American Saddlebreds. I was shocked when I saw what they did with the feet of these horses. They were grown out to a length treble normal and standing straight up as if they were on stilts. I asked what this was for, and they said that it was to encourage them to pick their feet up higher with each stride. Do you agree with this form of foot care?

Answer

Absolutely not. When I was young and still working with my father, I was asked to show American Saddlebred gaited horses for a particular client. I did it, and I loved the horses that I showed. They were generous and cooperative. I won major championships in the gaited horse division, but not a day passed without my questioning the way they were shod.

Every time I raised this question, I got the same answer. I was told that it was necessary to do it that way or one couldn't win. I recall saying over and over again, 'Why don't they change their rules?' Obviously I was never given an appropriate answer to this question.

Today much is being done to move gaited horses away from the extreme measures of the past. I love competition, and of course, it is fun to win; but I think we owe a responsibility to our horses to create conditions within our competitive efforts that are respectful to the health, welfare and comfort of the wonderful animals we regard as our partners.

GYMKHANA

Many young people find their way into the horse industry through having fun with gymkhana events. There's a way to win and still be fair to the horses that carry one to these victories. Winning is a lot more fun when you know that you have been reasonable with the mount that has so willingly carried you to victory.

I am a regular attendee at the Horse of the Year Show, now held in Birmingham. I enjoy the Pony Club Games as much as anyone does. It is, however, true that many of the competitors have placed a much higher priority on winning than they have on the fair treatment of the ponies they ride. It would not be fair to blame England or the Pony Club, as this is pretty much the case worldwide. Australia has a very active gymkhana division of the Pony Club; barrel racing and gymkhana events are huge in the United States. It just so happens that I probably see more gymkhanas in England than I do in any other country.

The creation of a set of rules that address the fair treatment of the ponies involved would be a wonderful project for the UK Pony Club to take on. It is certainly not true that harsh treatment is pervasive in gymkhana, but any that occurs is too much.

The very nature of gymkhana events sets up a scenario for harsh treatment, as success is all down to speed: whoever gets there first is the winner, and there is little attention paid to how it's done. If harsh treatment could bring about disqualification, contestants would come into compliance within a very short time.

It is my opinion that the barrel-racing associations in the USA are the greatest offenders when it comes to harsh treatment of gymkhana horses. I have been active in supporting rule changes, which have been effective in reducing inappropriate activity within these competitions. There is still work to do, but significant progress has been observed.

Question 110

What do I do with my gymkhana horse that refuses to enter the arena?

Answer

This is a question that comes to me from almost every group of people I address. A gymkhana is a unique activity. It is virtually the only equestrian contest where the horse is encouraged to run into the arena at top speed. This itself is a technique that encourages undesirable behaviour. Consider that the gymkhana horse is often asked to run full out into the arena, blast through a prescribed course and then run out of the arena as fast as possible, often while being whipped.

Having left the arena, the gymkhana horse often has its mouth jerked on hard to bring it to a stop. Then after waiting around for a while, the rider will ride towards the arena to ask the horse to do it again. Horses are not stupid. Why should the horse want to repeat an activity that is from his perspective painful and no fun at all? It amazes me how cooperative most gymkhana horses are under the circumstances.

In considering what follows, I would like the reader to understand that there are several gymkhana events that essentially fall into this category. For the gymkhana trainer and rider alike, I would like to recommend these same procedures, though it will be necessary for them to tailor the course pattern according to the activity in question.

It is my recommendation that the courses used in training sessions for gymkhana horses should be set up so that one can repeat procedures in a non-stop fashion. The horse should be brought into the arena in a calm and quiet fashion and should be ridden at a walk for a few minutes. Then the schooling process should begin, continuing in a constant ongoing pattern.

Any given course should be set up so that as you complete it you could simply begin a repetition of the first effort. You should execute the second course, and then return without stopping to the first course. The schooling session might be done at the walk, trot, canter and full gallop. I recommend that the usual speed pattern be reversed, ending your training session in a walk.

At the end of the session, the horse's adrenaline should be allowed to subside fully. I recommend that you dismount in the centre of the arena and either sit on the ground or walk with the horse for several minutes to completely disengage the horse from the training process. After you have accomplished this, then lead the horse out of the arena.

If it is possible to vary the gates used in the training sessions, this is desirable. The gymkhana trainer should pause to consider how long it takes to train a horse to run out through the arena gate. I suggest that this can be accomplished in one or two training sessions and should in no way be a part of the daily training routine.

Whipping the gymkhana horse is highly overrated as a means of increasing speed. I have been impressed in recent years to see that many gymkhana competitors are using a short piece of rope fixed to the saddle horn, which they flick back and forth in front of them to encourage the horse to run faster. This seldom inflicts pain and is far more effective than a burning whip. The gymkhana world desperately needs to learn this lesson of being more respectful of their four-legged partners.

Recommended additional resource: 1

SHOW JUMPERS, HUNTERS AND OTHER COMPETITION HORSES

This division represents the largest segment of competitive riders on a global basis. In show jumping, the horse is asked for a supreme effort. The needs of that animal should be met and addressed if one is to expect a willing performance.

As a child, I was very active in the world of show jumping and working hunters over fences in the United States. I witnessed training techniques that would get you arrested today. This competitive world has changed dramatically, and in my opinion mostly for the better; but there is still work to do.

I believe that we should take a hard look at the aspect of timing horses over fences, causing them to jump at breakneck speeds. It seems to me that this is inviting training methods that I would consider harsh and unnecessary. Obviously, the rules we have in place need to be enforced more effectively than they have been, and our associations should undertake to bring this about.

Question 111

Why does my horse refuse a jump?

Answer

Probably, you have overmatched him at some point. Get the fences lower, let him have fun and rebuild his confidence. Elevate the fences gradually, attempting to discover his maximum capability. Horses don't simply refuse a jump for no reason. If I ask you if he has ever refused a cavalletti, I believe your response would be 'No'. If that's the case, then a simple answer is that the fence was too high.

Obviously, that simple answer may not be the whole story. It could be that the fence was scary, and he had never seen it before. It's possible that the ground was too slippery or the going too deep. There are many reasons why a horse may refuse a jump. With that in mind, however, one should realize that horses are generous animals and willing workers. If the environment is set up properly, they love to jump. It is a natural activity with them.

My statement that the horse was probably overmatched is a well-founded general explanation for a horse stopping at a fence. To qualify ourselves as good horsepeople, we should take a hard look at all of the factors involved, come to a conclusion and act in the best interest of the horse to solve his problem. Lowering the fence will be one of the answers in a high percentage of cases involving refusal.

When we are acting responsibly with our horse, we will work to set up a scenario in which he feels good about successfully jumping a fence, and then reward him appropriately. One of the most effective rewards I have used is to have the fence high enough for the horse to feel achievement in jumping it, while still low enough for him to accept. If the rider dismounts as soon as the horse has negotiated the fence, leads him around and allows him to feel pleased with himself in having accomplished his feat, that horse will be a more willing partner.

If you are clever about this, you can arrange your training programme so that the schooling session for any given day is conducted over fences that are educational but not overly taxing. Once you have accomplished this, then you can ask the horse to tackle a fence that is a bit of a challenge, ensuring that he approaches it going in his favourite direction; you can then accomplish the jump, dismount and finish the day's session on a positive note.

You can play with this scenario until you reach what is generally fairly obvious as the horse's physical limit. Through this method, you can optimize the performance of your horse. However, a good horseperson will observe the horse's responses carefully and be very careful about increasing the demand.

Question 112

You work mostly on horse problems such as biting, kicking or refusing to go into the trailer. Do you think your methods could make top horses even more successful, get dressage horses more concentrated in the arena or make show jumpers show more spirit in the course? Have you ever been successful in working with top sport dressage or show jumping horses?

Answer

When you create a partnership with your horse, causing the horse to do his work because he wants to and not because he is forced to, then you improve the performance of that horse no matter what the discipline is.

I have worked with dressage horses for both Camilla du Pont and Charlotte Bredahl. Charlotte, who was an Olympic bronze medal winner in Barcelona, used my methods and has a horse in training with me at the moment.

At one time my partner Jeff Lovinger and I owned a wonderful Thoroughbred who didn't make it to the racetrack, so we put him in a hunter/jumper programme on my farm. Now deceased, Napur became one of the world's best show jumpers for several years and was shown by Hap Hansen and Will Simpson in both the United States and Europe.

Rough Frolic led the United States for several years as a hunter and was one of the most successful in that division. It happens that Rough Frolic retired early from racing and went on to be what is known as a strip hunter in the United States. These are judged on conformation as well as performance.

These are not the only two top competition jumpers that I worked with, but they are the most noteworthy.

However, please do not think that any equestrian discipline is unique. Where horses are concerned, the similarities far outweigh the differences, regardless of the breed, the size or the activity. A horse is a horse, and the needs of these animals are not limited to particular disciplines.

I have ridden eight World Champions in the show ring. While all these were in the Western division, I also showed many hunters and jumpers and won one national championship in the saddle, which involved hunters, jumpers and Western horses. I can state categorically that the general needs of the horses in each of these disciplines are quite similar. To achieve high performance from the cutting horse, reining horse, hunter or jumper, certain elements of cooperation must be accomplished. It matters not what the discipline is.

Probably the most important horses of the latter half of my career have been on the racetracks of the world, and I can tell you beyond a shadow of a doubt the same elements are important there as in the above-mentioned disciplines. I have been fortunate to work with over four hundred international stakes winners in racing competition. I had 'Horse of the World' two separate years. Those individuals needed the concepts I have discovered as much as any of my cutting horses or reined cow horses did.

Recommended additional resources: 1, 6

WESTERN DIVISION

This is an activity that is growing very rapidly on the world scene. It has recently been included in the Olympic movement, and many feel that it will soon grow at an even greater rate. My early years were spent most heavily involved in the Western division of equestrian competition. I showed cutting horses, reining horses, Western pleasure, Western trail and roping horses, and competed in 'Western Riding', which is a Western version of dressage.

I personally feel that working cattle from horseback is the most exciting form of riding on earth. Europe and the UK are coming to understand the Western riding technique better and better every year. It is gratifying for me to watch a good Western horse in England, Germany or Italy. Some of the horses based in these countries are competing very well in the world arena.

Question 113

My Western horse's gait is rough. How can I appear to have a good seat in the show ring?

Answer

There are two major factors involved when it comes to presenting a pleasing appearance on a Western horse while sitting at the trot. They are the gait of the horse and the ability of the rider. There is a third minor facet, and that is the equipment used.

While the gait of the horse is his inherent property, there are things we can do to modify it. When a Western horse trots in a rough, pounding fashion, he is typically far worse the faster you trot. If one can concentrate on training your horse to trot very slowly, the roughness is reduced dramatically.

The rider can improve a look of the trot by carefully studying all of the factors involved in sitting smoothly while trotting. The rider's ankles usually play a significant role in acting as shock absorbers at this gait. The knees, thigh muscles and certainly waist and upper body can all be trained to provide a judge with a more aesthetically pleasing picture.

Equipment, while a relatively minor factor, can also come into play in an effort to cause the trot to look smoother. A very low cantle will generally accentuate the bouncing motion of the rider's posterior. A saddle that is slightly more elevated front and rear will help a rider to appear more comfortably nestled at the trot. Loose clothing with fringy projections would tend to accentuate the trot. Even the hairdo will sometimes magnify the roughness of the horse's gait or cause it to seem smoother.

A Western saddle that has a deep, softly padded seat will allow for a smoother-looking ride than a sleek, hard leather one. One should be sure that all loose saddle strings and/or other appointments to the saddle are firmly fixed in place so that you see less movement as you view the overall picture.

One should be ever mindful of the fact that a firm, fit, healthy human body is far easier to present as attractive while riding than a body that is out of shape. Fitness has nothing but positives to offer humans and horses alike. Fit individuals tend to live longer and have healthier and happier lives.

Question 114

How long do you train your reining horses before showing in competition?

Answer

Most of the world-class trainers that I have known would answer this question in a fairly similar fashion to how I will answer it. It is very difficult to expect a horse to execute the procedures necessary for competition with less than one full year of training. Even at that level the reining horse should still be considered a baby. It is my opinion that after one year's training any competition should be limited to very few competitive events. A sustained schedule of competitions after just one year's training will generally result in a resentful horse.

I consider two to three years to be optimum in maximizing the performance of the reining horse. Even after three years, the reined horse is apt to continue to improve if trained with good horsemanship. Most reined horses reach their full potential at the age of eight to nine years.

TRAVEL AND WORK ON THE ROAD

You would have to conclude that my work is a mission with me. No entirely sane human being could possibly keep my schedule without being driven by an enormous desire from within to create change. It is my belief that our horses deserve it.

Since 1989, when Her Majesty Queen Elizabeth II first saw my work and endorsed it, I have completed over sixteen hundred public demonstrations. With a lot of luck and blessed by good health, I have not missed one or been late for one to this date. I have concluded that if I am to change the mindset of the equine world, I must go to the horsepeople; they will not come to me, at least not in sufficient numbers to make a difference. Travel, especially in recent years, is far from fun, but I enjoy what happens when I get there, so I feel the upside outweighs the downside.

Question 115

Do you still go to England to visit and work with the Queen's horses?

Answer

Yes, in fact, England is on my current schedule for two months of every year. While I tour the country to do demonstrations, each visit will include at least one stop involving Her Majesty and the horses of the royal family. So far I have made something close to thirty trips involving the Queen and the Queen's horses. However, these are directed more at the people involved in training horses for the royal family than for the horses themselves. Her Majesty continues to be vitally interested in my getting my message to as many horsepeople as possible, and certainly this includes those who train and care for the royal stables.

Her Majesty's interests include an incredibly wide range of horses and disciplines. There are those horses that are kept for personal rides virtually daily, as well as those that race. The native ponies of Scotland have become very popular with the royal family, and many of these ponies have been seen winning championships at major English horse shows for decades now. Her Majesty has often stated publicly that her favourite family of horses involves three generations of coloured Warmbloods: Tinkerbell, Peter Pan and Tiger Lily, who make up one of the most attractive lines of coloured horses one could ever imagine.

My association with Her Majesty continues to be one of the most exciting aspects of my entire career. It is my opinion that my message would have been far more difficult to disseminate to the world in the absence of the Queen's endorsement than it was with it. Terry Pendry, stud groom to Her Majesty, continues to be of great help to me when getting my message across within the royal stables and also out to the rest of the world.

Question 116

Mr Roberts, do you still travel to give lectures? Do you talk to schools and companies as you used to?

Answer

My travel schedule would rival that of an airline pilot. They tell me that I logged well over two hundred thousand miles in 2006. It appears as though 2007 will be no exception in this long list of years in which I have covered more than one hundred thousand miles in each twelvemonth.

I have been doing more speaking to corporate groups in the past three years, and am now addressing about thirty a year. My work to get my message across in schools has also increased in intensity – in fact, I deal with the education of children almost as much as I deal with training horses these days.

Prisons and their needs have been high on my priorities list for decades now. It is difficult to schedule visits to prisons because of the many regulations and restrictions, but I particularly enjoy assisting those who have lost their way a bit. They need help just as remedial horses do.

Youth detention centres and women's prisons seem to get more out of my time and energy than adult men's prisons do. I will accept the challenge of a men's institution, but I feel far more productive when dealing with ladies and children. Some day I would love to write a book about my experiences with this segment of our society.

Question 117

At seventy-two years of age, how can you possibly handle the schedule that we read about on your website? It would seem impossible that you can change continents, time zones, and even hemispheres with the pace that is evident on your website.

Answer

I have been very fortunate to study and become familiar with four natural substances which have allowed me to keep up a schedule that would wear down most people in their thirties:

1.   melatonin
2.   co-enzyme Q-10
3.   Transfer Factor™
4.   oligomeric proanthocyanidins

Melatonin allows me to sleep five to six hours in what is termed REM sleep (the deepest kind). For me, sleep occurs about thirty minutes after putting a small tablet under my tongue. It contains 2.5 mg of melatonin. This is a natural substance, but you should check with a doctor before trying it to be sure you are not likely to experience any negative side effects. I have experienced no negatives with my use of melatonin and have taken it every night of my life since 1991.

Co-enzyme Q-10 (CoQ10) this again is a natural substance, generally derived from fish. It has but one obligation, and that is to increase the oxygen in your bloodstream. I take 100mg per day after breakfast. CoQ10 is size conscious, so Pat takes 60 mg per day. Our bodies require oxygen to heal and to fend off invaders of one sort or another. Without oxygen, we are sitting targets for viruses and other organisms. In the presence of highly oxygenated blood, we have a much better defence mechanism.

Transfer Factor™ is a relatively new discovery. It is the heart and soul of colostrum. This means that the first milk of mammals (cows in this instance) is broken down so that only the factor for the enhancement of the immune system is present. The world will come to know that this substance, found in most female mammals for approximately forty-eight hours after giving birth, is one of the most important elements where enhancing our immune system is concerned. Most of the colostrum used in this process is derived from organic dairies in the beautiful grassy country of New Zealand. These dairy farms use no fertilizer, spray or medicines in connection with the cows that produce this colostrum. If a cow requires medication, she is removed from the programme. These dairy cows produce nearly a hundred times the colostrum that they require for their own calves, so while their needs are met, there is ample available for the necessary processing to achieve Transfer Factor.

Oligomeric proanthocyanidins (OPCs) are the result of decades of study worldwide. The object of this research was to obtain certain substances containing antioxidants. The first real success occurred in France and was an extraction of pine bark. Later, through a massive amount of work, the process was perfected with the seeds of red grapes. At this point in time OPCs are being gathered from several other botanical sources, including bilberry seeds, citrus seeds, cranberry seeds and others.

I believe that the addition of this substance to the three above has resulted in a significant positive change in my life. I began using OPCs in September 2001, and I have the distinct impression that my ability to fend off illnesses has been greatly enhanced as a result. I am of the opinion that the addition of OPCs to my diet has also been responsible for an incredible improvement in my memory skills. I could give many examples, but suffice it to say the improvement has been dramatic.

I have asked that an article written by my wife, Pat, be published in my quarterly *Join-Up Journal* as well as on our website. It describes how, for approximately fifteen years now, I have been following a schedule that would be considered overwhelming by virtually any-one's standards. Among other things, you will see that I have completed more than sixteen hundred individual demonstration events without missing, cancelling or even being late for one of the performances. On many trips virtually my whole team has come down with a flu or cold bug of one sort or another. Often I felt these bugs enter my system; incredibly I was 100 per cent successful at kicking them out within a matter of two to five hours. This experience has been profound.

SINGLE-LINE LUNGEING

It is my strong belief that single-line lungeing is the second worst piece of horsemanship on earth – second only to striking a horse to produce pain. I know this is a bitter pill for many people, but if you consider the matter properly, you can only conclude that I am right.

In demonstrations, I consistently show how horses that have been single-line lunged for significant amounts of time are truly habituated to a pattern of travel that is injurious to mind and body. Every horse that is single-line lunged for more than thirty days or so will travel with its head to the outside of the circle. This one act sets the pattern for complete anatomical malfunction.

Once the head is outside the circle of travel, the spine must then take a curve opposite to the circumference of the circle on which the horse is travelling. When the spine is curved inappropriately, then the pelvis attachment and the shoulders are acting in an uncoordinated fashion. What this means is that the two main muscle masses of the horse's anatomy are working one against the other, while they should be assisting one another in a harmonious effort.

Question 118

Why do you dislike single-line lungeing?

Answer

Single-line lungeing places the horse's body completely out of balance. With a single line attached to its head, the horse will eventually travel with its head to the outside of the circle. It will consequently tend to arc its back in the opposite curve to that traced by the circle it is following.

At the canter, most horses that are single-line lunged will tend to cross lead or travel disunited. I give demonstrations where I show how to help horses that are the victims of single-line lungeing, and I can improve their body position dramatically in thirty to forty minutes.

I use a surcingle with side reins that have elastic in them. Schooling the horse to travel with his head directly in front or slightly

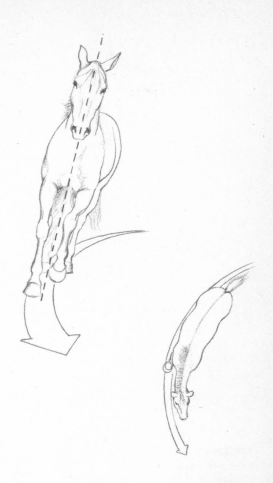

118.1 This shows the natural head and neck position of a horse in a circle, without the single line.

inward to the circle, I gradually tighten the side reins until I achieve bilateral symmetry. At this point I put two lines on the horse so that I eliminate the weight of one line attached to the horse's head. With two lines, I can easily control the rear leads so that the horse does not travel disunited.

Worldwide, the act of single-line lungeing is causing problems for horses, requiring chiropractors and therapists to treat these animals routinely so that they can travel without pain. Single-line lungeing

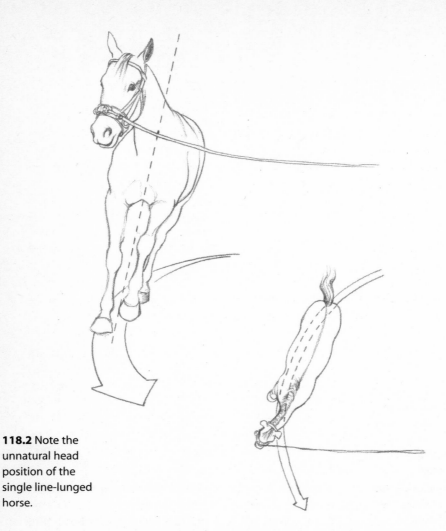

118.2 Note the unnatural head position of the single line-lunged horse.

causes significant pain to hundreds of thousands of horses every day.

This problem has been so important to me that I have devoted a major chapter to it in my textbook. I have included there several diagrams that illustrate the way in which single-line lungeing causes the unbalanced conditions that I have described briefly in this answer.

ASK MONTY • MONTY ROBERTS

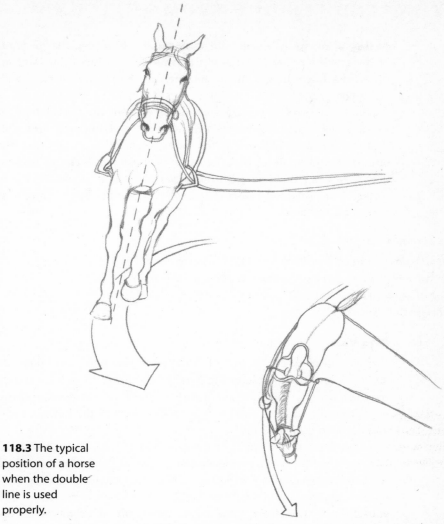

118.3 The typical position of a horse when the double line is used properly.

Lungeing in the fashion that I have recommended here is easy to accomplish and far healthier for your horse.

Recommended additional resource: 1

BITING AND FEEDING FROM THE HAND

At this point, we will deal with what I call the third worst piece of horsemanship on earth. This is true unless, of course, you want to teach your horse to bite. If you do, then feeding from the hand will assist you greatly.

There are ways to reward your horse without the use of food. I recommend a good rub between the eyes and walking away; one will find that the horse will tend to follow and regard this act as a friendly one. It should be noted that 'no blade of grass has ever run from a horse', so it is simply not logical to expect a horse to regard food as a trophy. Once the food is associated with the human body, biting is a logical consequence.

Question 119

I regularly do groundwork with my horse. Can I when he is working cooperatively give him some small rewards (food or horse treats) during training, or does the horse have to wait until the training ends for this kind of reward?

Answer

If this kind of reward is to be offered by the human hand, then he should wait throughout eternity. Feeding the horse from the hand is the third worst piece of horsemanship on earth. Horses do not regard food from the hand as reward, but connect food to the human body and thus are trained to bite.

In my textbook, there is a chapter on dealing with horses that bite. Much of it is devoted to my belief that it is wrong to feed horses from the hand. It explains that horses do not have to stalk their food, so they do not consider it a reward. Your horse will be much better behaved if you do not feed from your hand. Read up on better ways to congratulate your horse.

Recommended additional resource: 1

Question 120

My mother-in-law, Pauline, has recently bought a six-year-old Quarter Horse named Guy. She's a novice rider, just learning the ropes and obviously getting to know Guy's little 'habits'. He's once or twice tried to nip her, much to her surprise (she's a very gentle woman, loves animals and would never ever take her hand to anything). Her 'stable mates' have told her to hit him every time he does this. After reading your books, we thought you were best qualified to give us some answers. What should she do to stop him?

Answer

Thank you for taking the time to inquire for your mother-in-law. It is not clear in your email whether she feeds her new horse from the hand. This is one of the most common mistakes made by horse owners in the world today. Many people hold the mistaken assumption that feeding treats will cause your horse to want to be with you and encourage affection. In fact, it causes your horse to want to be with your treat, not you, and, if you are in the way, they will nip or bite you!

If this is indeed the case, please encourage your mother-in-law to stop feeding Guy treats, and make sure no one else is feeding him from the hand either. If she wishes to give him carrots or apples, that is fine, but put them on the ground or in the feed bin rather than offering them on her hand. A horse is a prey animal, and as such does not see food as a 'trophy' in the same way as a predator would.

Your mother-in-law is correct in her feeling that she should not raise her hand to Guy. I have worked with hundreds, possibly thousands, of horses that bite, and I have found a very simple and effective solution. When Guy reaches to bite Pauline, she needs to bump him lightly on the shin of his leg with her foot. I am *not* encouraging her to strike Guy to cause pain. What I am endeavouring to do is cause Guy's attention to be shifted from his thoughts of biting to his leg. This is a form of behaviour habituation, and within six to eight repetitions you will see that Guy moves to nip and then looks down at his leg. This training will tend to achieve a behavioural shift within a short period of time.

It is important that Pauline is consistent with her training with Guy, i.e. that she remembers to re-train that behaviour every time she sees it recur. It is also important that she be aware of Guy's personal space and respect it. It is appropriate for us to expect our horses to be respectful of our space and not push us with their heads, rub against our shoulders or nip us. Conversely, Guy should expect the same respect from your mother-in-law. Pauline needs to be conscious when she is working around Guy, and when she is standing and holding him while she chats to someone. She needs to ensure that there is enough space for him to comfortably relax his head and body without having to avoid bumping into her.

Recommended additional resource: 1

LOADING, VEHICLES AND TRANSPORTATION

This is the number one remedial problem with horses on earth, and one that I believe I deal with more effectively than any other that I meet. It is a challenge for a majority of horsepeople worldwide, but one with relatively easy solutions if people will choose to seek them out.

Walk through the following questions with me, think through my recommendations and try them on your horses, and I believe that you will put an end to trailer loading and travelling problems. If I were to come up with a list of remedial problems in the order in which I am most likely to succeed, then trailer loading would be at the top of that list.

Question 121

We are buying a horse trailer with living quarters and were wondering if you could comment on the pros and cons of mangers.

Answer

It is important to take into consideration the purpose for which you are acquiring a trailer. Obviously if you are a professional travelling a thousand miles a week or so and basically living on the road, then you and your horses have an entirely different set of requirements from the horseman who travels to the occasional trail ride or short distances to horse shows.

There is nothing wrong with mangers. My assumption in formulating this answer is that we are discussing slant haul trailers. If you decide to include mangers, then it is best to choose a trailer with wider stalls. If you choose to put mangers in a narrower trailer and you have full-sized horses, you could restrict their space unacceptably.

For the hard-travelling professional, mangers provide several advantages. They make it easier for you to feed and water your horses while on the move and, in addition, they allow for significantly more storage space than trailers without mangers as most trailers will utilize the space below the manger for extra storage. I am a spokesman for several types of trailers on a global basis and many companies produce a manger that is safe and effective.

Be very careful to use only mangers that are built from extremely strong material and constructed so that they have no areas that could injure a horse's leg. All edges should be smooth, and all flat portions should be reinforced so that your horse cannot tear the metal. Many injuries occur when time and use has weakened the metal and cracks occur. Cracks in metal can be like a knife to the flesh of your horse.

The feed compartment of a manger need not be more than 5 or 6 inches in depth and should have an outward sloping lip on the rise closest to your horse. This construction will allow the horse to pull his foot out of the manger if he is silly enough to get it in there.

You are probably aware that I am a strong proponent of slant haul trailers. If you have read my textbook, you will be aware that I recommend partial partitions. I have also stated that I am a strong proponent of ramps as opposed to step-up trailers. Some of my companies produce trailers in accordance with my specifications.

Recommended additional resource: 1

Question 122

I have a five-year-old Quarter Horse mare that I have used your Join-Up with to the best of my ability. However, when I load her on the trailer she is fine until I close the gate; then she panics, even if I have my old mare on with her who is very quiet in the trailer. I have a three-horse slant load 2006 Sundowner that is 7 feet, 7 inches, as I transport Standardbreds as well, so it is not small. There are windows, but she tends to act claustrophobic. She starts to shake and sweat, and then she explodes. I have taken time to load her and feed her on the trailer; she stands with me on the trailer, but as soon as I close the gate she rears up, paws and kicks – the whole thing. When I go in to get her, she stands quiet, lets me undo her tie, walks out with me a little shaky, but she will turn right around and load again. I think she is just very afraid! Do you have any suggestions that I could use to help her learn not to be so afraid?

Answer

I must say that this is one of the most interesting questions I have had come to me in the past year or so. The primary reason I find it so interesting is that I am reading the words of someone who concerns himself with the necessity to be fair with the horse before making conclusions. I love to hear that you reached out to provide a slant haul trailer, and I am impressed that you have provided the headspace that might otherwise have contributed to this condition.

It is extremely interesting that even though you have experienced explosive behaviour when the door closes, this mare will allow you to come in and handle her comfortably after you have opened the door. This particular behavioural shift is not often apparent. Usually, once the frantic behaviour has begun, it is a considerable length of time before any quiet cooperation is evident.

It is also true that this sort of problem is generally found in the yearling or two-year-old who has yet to take on the maturity of the adult horse. It would be nice to know how many times you have experienced this activity, but I wouldn't say it was critical to the recommendation that I intend to make.

Let's just stop for a moment and ask yourself if you think it would ever be possible to transport this mare quietly and comfortably with the door closed. I believe that your answer would be that you think it would, but she would probably have to be a lot older and more experienced with travel before it could ever happen.

Let's take the position that, with this in mind, we are talking about positive experiences during transportation with doors closed. Bearing this in mind, I would suggest that you borrow, if you don't have one, a stock trailer or just an old trailer that somebody hauls cows around in without partitions and with a non-skid floor. I suggest that you put three or four horses in the trailer with her.

If it were a 14-foot stock trailer, you would probably want three horses with her. If it is a sixteen-footer or bigger, you could transport her with four partners. If it's possible to use horses she is familiar with, this would be preferable to transporting her with unfamiliar individuals. You should take precautions against any of the horses getting kicked by having a sufficient number to limit the space around them. In other words, if the horses are close together, it is virtually impossible for them to damage one another by kicking. If there are large spaces between the horses, then a powerful kick is quite possible.

Each horse should be free to roam the trailer untied. It is amazing how horses will school bad behaviour better than any human being could. Once all the horses are loaded and the door is closed, you should begin to roll at once. It is not a good idea to allow the horses to stand in a motionless trailer for more than a few minutes. Once you are rolling, then it is advisable to take a fairly long trip. It is my opinion that your mare will tend to settle within half an hour or so.

Many stock trailers are open to a certain extent. Generally the sides and rear have spaces between panels of about 4 to 6 inches, allowing the light and air to come through. If this is the case, then once your mare has settled well to a trip in the trailer, you should repeat the process having covered these open areas to exclude the light. It is possible that you will have to repeat this process more than once before attempting to transport in your normal trailer again.

Should you get good results with the stock trailer but less than wonderful behaviour in the slant haul, then take out one partition and try your mare with a double-width stall. After several trips with this configuration, then give it a go with the fully closed trailer and a familiar horse as company.

Recommended additional resource: 1

Question 123

I recently acquired a six-year-old mustang mare. I was told she trailered well, but she walked right up to the trailer and stopped. She didn't act scared, but when we tried again she went right up, stopped and sat with her rump right on the ground. We chuckled about it and after a few seconds she snorted, got up and walked right in. She does this every time. While this doesn't hurt her, it would be nice if she would walk in without sitting first. Any suggestions would be helpful. I do not know much about her past; she's a rescue.

Answer

It sounds as though you could have a very funny act on your hands. She is obviously quite stressed with the prospect of loading and travelling. This could be the result of negative experiences in her past. To assist her, you will need repeatedly to create situations that will be comfortable so as to reduce the stress level by reinforcing in her mind the belief that trailers and travel can be safe and comfortable.

Apparently your mare has figured out how to control the situation. I would school your mare to respect the Dually halter. Once this is accomplished, she will choose to load without sitting down.

The Dually is designed to allow the horse to train itself to come up off the halter willingly when a request is made. There is a specific set of procedures that must be accomplished before the horse is likely to act in a cooperative manner. DVDs describing procedures are extremely helpful, but there is no substitute for practice in becoming proficient with any piece of equipment with which you intend to train a horse. I often say that the Dually halter is no better than the hands that hold it, and the way to get the hands better is to have them practise its use.

I recommend strongly that every horseperson work with easy, cooperative horses before progressing to those more difficult. As one becomes better with the easy horses, each procedure will tend to educate both you and your muscles to make the right moves in order to achieve the desired result.

Recommended additional resources: 1, 5

Question 124

Do you recommend tying your horse in a trailer?

Answer

Sure, I recommend that you tie your horse in the trailer – for several reasons. One reason is that if you have to stop very suddenly and the horse happens to have his head down between his front legs, he could be injured. Do not over-restrict your horse; the tie needs only to be short enough to keep him from dropping his head down between his front legs.

Any time a question comes to me about tying a horse in the trailer, I want to include in my answer the following statement: *never tie your horse up in the trailer until you have a secure closure behind him.* One of the great surprises I had in store for me at the time that I went public with my first book and my demonstration was that people break this rule.

My entire career up to that point was as a professional with horses on the road in competition, and I didn't see people making this mistake very often. Now that I deal with the general public, I find that it is much more common than I realized. It is an extremely dangerous practice, and destroys many horses each year. The lives and limbs of people are also in jeopardy when this rule is broken.

When a horse is tied in a narrow place with nothing securing him from the rear, he is called upon by all inherent tendencies to pull back if he meets the tether with no rear restrictions. Once a horse is pulling back while inside a trailer, disastrous circumstances begin to occur. If it's a step-up trailer, he generally gets his hind legs outside and then under the trailer. If it's a ramp, his hind legs reach a lower level, and he generally bangs his head on the ceiling of the trailer. Injuries and even death often result.

Setting that fact aside, even if there were no physical damage, the psychological damage to the horse would still be incredibly serious. Horses will become 'fly-back' artists because of this experience, and when a horse exits a trailer at extreme speeds people can be injured, or worse, and the horses can suffer injury too.

At my demonstrations, I try to answer as many questions as possible. Many of the questions I am asked pertain to trailer problems. When someone comes up and says, 'My horse goes in the trailer just fine,' I am relatively sure at this point that they have either a horse that fights the walls or one that flies back out of the trailer. If it's a fly-back artist, then I am virtually certain that someone has tied the horse up without rear closure.

There is a procedure for dealing with fly-back artists, but I will reserve that for the specific question pertaining to this remedial behaviour.

Question 125

My seven-year-old horse flies backward out of the trailer every time. I have owned him for over three years now and nothing negative that I know of has happened to him during this time concerning trailers. The former owner told me that he once had the bar against his leg. I am sure that he still fears it will happen again when he has to get out of the trailer. How can I take away that fear completely and forever? I would like him to enjoy the drive on the trailer without having him blast like a rocket out of it.

Answer

This could very well be the most important question included in this book. Flying out of the trailer backwards is extremely dangerous behaviour that I have to deal with very often. I recommend Join-Up and then the use of the Dually halter until the horse understands how to move forward off the Dually. After one achieves complete cooperation when schooling with the Dually halter, one can progress to the next step, which is to back the trailer towards a solid wall. Drop the ramp when the bottom of it will reach a point approximately 1 yard (1 metre) from the wall.

After placing the trailer in this position, I recommend placing two panels or gates in a position so that they become barriers extending from the wall to the trailer. Each panel will pass near one edge of the ramp. Walk the horse into the 1-metre area between the wall and the ramp and then swing your panel (or gate) over to meet the wall. Having accomplished this, the horse is in a small corral about 8 to 10 feet (around 3 metres) square.

Attach the panels to the trailer with a strong tie. If possible, attach the other end of each panel to the wall. At this point you are ready to walk your horse up the ramp toward the trailer. I recommend that you stop after about two steps and back up touching the wall with the horse's tail. This will register with the horse that there is a solid wall at that point. Continue the process of walking forward and backing up until the horse is completely in the trailer. It is essential to repeatedly reverse the horse until he touches the back wall even if there is a

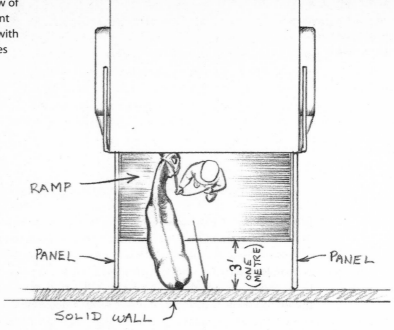

125.1 Overview of the environment set up to deal with a horse that flies back out of a trailer.

RAMP

PANEL

PANEL

3' (ONE METRE)

SOLID WALL

willingness on the part of the horse to walk straight into the trailer. This will imprint his brain to the fact that the wall is there should he opt to fly backwards while fully in the trailer.

One can walk into the vehicle and expect the horse to follow. In extreme cases, should the animal refuse to come forward, one can place tension on the Dually halter, and wait for the slightest motion forward by the horse. If forward motion is observed, be quick to reward it with a rub between the eyes. If the horse flies backwards, release the pressure, allowing the horse to reach the wall. Once the horse has bumped the wall and come to a complete stop, one should begin the pressure again on the Dually halter and wait to observe forward motion.

When the animal negotiates the ramp and enters the trailer, his work is just beginning. The horse should be backed out of the trailer and reloaded ten to fifteen times before making any changes to the

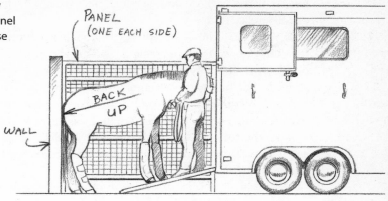

125.2 Side view with the rear panel removed for ease of viewing.

PANEL
(ONE EACH SIDE)

BACK UP

WALL

procedure. Once the horse is negotiating the loading and backing-out process with adrenaline down and in complete comfort, one can begin to remove the influence of the wings and walls. One can also move the vehicle to lessen the effect of the assistance provided by these objects. One should continue the process, changing the conditions only gradually, until the horse loads into and backs with ease out of a vehicle that is freestanding and without wings of any sort.

As with virtually every remedial problem we deal with, there will be times of relapse. You may have removed the panels and be getting along fine, and so begin the process of moving the trailer slightly further from the wall. At some point it is likely that the horse will once again fly back out of the trailer. When that happens, I recommend that the trailer be moved back to an area that the horse can handle, and that you once again start the process of gradually moving the trailer away from the wall.

These loading and backing-out procedures should take place at times when there is no need for travel. Waiting until you have to travel usually means you don't have enough time and patience to execute these procedures without anxiety. Each procedure described here should be conducted in a calm, cool and tranquil fashion.

It should be your goal to achieve willing loading with the adrenaline level of the horse as low as possible. The horse should walk quietly with his head low and exhibit licking and chewing, which denotes relaxation.

If you follow these procedures to the letter, the results are usually incredibly good. You can create a loader that will walk into the trailer on his own with very little effort. I often accept a horse for a demonstration that has been extremely difficult to load for years, and he generally negotiates the loading and backing-out process within a minute or two of the time that I actually ask him to load.

Take the time, keep your adrenaline level low and always regard safety as the number one priority. Remember: *never tie your horse in the trailer without secure closure behind him*.

I have given this same advice in other answers, but it is a rule so critical and so often broken that I feel I must take every opportunity to remind owners of it, in order to protect them from causing this dangerous remedial problem. Any time a horse flies back out of the trailer, it is a virtual certainty that the horse has been tied up before a secure closure is achieved behind him. When a horse pulls back in a narrow space and has no closure behind him, he is going to fight until either the rope breaks or he is down with potential injuries.

It is interesting that you point out in your question that the former owner indicated there might have been a problem with a bar behind the horse. It is most probable that the former owner made the grave error of tying up the horse before closing the trailer behind him. It is likely that, once having created this dangerous behaviour, embarrassment set in, discouraging the owner from explaining what actually happened.

As I travel the world, I find that loading is the number one remedial problem everywhere, and that a large percentage of these problems involve the red-letter rule that I have outlined in this answer having been broken. *Never tie your horse in the trailer without secure closure behind him*. Please be diligent with the recommendations I have given you, and your horse will soon be able to leave the trailer calmly, and you will be able to prevent this problem with other horses in the future.

Recommended additional resources: 1, 3, 5, 9

ASK MONTY • MONTY ROBERTS

REMEDIAL GROOMING

In considering the subject of this section, horsepeople are required to stop and consider the historical circumstances that have created this problem. Once these are established, then solutions are quite easy to come by.

When horses express anger with the act of grooming, it is likely that someone has been inappropriately harsh in carrying it out. The person may not even know that they acted harshly – maybe the equipment was the culprit; but the horse finds it difficult to disassociate the equipment from the human.

It is critical that we closely observe every aspect of our interaction with the horses with which we deal. With remedial grooming problems, close observation will virtually always expose an inappropriately painful act or article of grooming equipment.

Question 126

I have just acquired a nice seven-year-old ex-racehorse Thoroughbred mare. She is very sane, quiet and also seven months pregnant. My problem is that she does not like to be groomed. She will pin her ears back and threaten with her back legs. She gnashes her teeth and attempts to bite when I brush her. Help.

Answer

It is inspiring that you are working with an ex-racehorse, as it is vitally important that these horses are given the chance to re-train and be useful partners after their racing careers are over. Please be aware that many ex-racehorses have become wonderful pleasure horses and even champions in competition.

If you have ever seen racehorses being groomed at the racetrack, you will notice that the horses are tied very short and high on the back wall of a box stall. One can easily imagine how this process might create a horse that is highly resentful of being groomed. The concepts inherent in the language *Equus* are based upon the premise of always giving the horse the power of choice. Horses will react to any given procedure according to their level of comfort throughout the experience.

It is important to realize that Thoroughbred horses are inherently thin-skinned and sensitive to the touch. This may not be extreme for many of them, but I can assure you that it is critical to a high percentage. At the racetrack professional grooms tend to disregard this sensitivity, tether them high on the wall and groom harshly while standing in a position where they can't be kicked or bitten.

My suggestion to you is that you change your grooming habits dramatically. Give a lot of baths and eliminate the brushing. Use a cloth to rub your horse's body when the hair is dry after a bath. Repeat the process with the cloth many times so that the horse comes to know that the grooming process can be painless.

If you can do Join-Up and cause the horse to want to be with you, this will be valuable. You will form a closer relationship with your horse, which will assist you in stopping her aggressive behaviour toward you. I also recommend schooling to the Dually halter so that you can create a horse that knows the value of standing still. School with the Dually, backing your horse up when she is negative and leaving the Dually alone when she is positive.

These remedial problems can be a lot of fun to work with if you take up the challenge to learn the language of your horse and create an attitude within your mind that you will work with her in the absence of pain and violence.

We should be ever mindful of the fact that sensitive horses are often the high achievers. They tend to respond to our directions more quickly and generously than horses that lack sensitivity. This is not a major problem to overcome when you get your work right and respond to your horse in a respectful manner.

Recommended additional resources: 1, 3, 5

GIRTHY (CINCH-BOUND) HORSES

This is an area filled with danger for horses and horsepeople alike. It is incumbent upon all of us to learn about this phenomenon and seek solutions to it. The phenomenon of the cinch-bound or girthy horse can be exceedingly dangerous for both horse and human. Many horses have suffered major injuries and even death as a result of this odd characteristic embedded deeply in the psyche of some individuals.

It is my hope that this section will assist many horsepeople in understanding the unique aspects of horses that are cinch-bound and bad to saddle. If I am successful, I will effectively save many horses and people from exposure to a significant danger.

Within the genes of all horses there is a tendency to move into pressure. This has been discussed in other sections of this book, notably in the context of horses that pull back, but the cinch-bound horse typically expresses the tendency particularly violently. A horse that is cinch-bound will react to a tight girth by becoming rigid, elevating the back and then tending to fly backwards, collapsing the rear quarters.

The end result of this reaction can often be a back flip, which can result in a fractured skull, a broken saddle and, if a person is trapped under the animal, extreme injuries or even death for them. It is highly important for these reasons never to tack up the cinch-bound horse while it is tied. This act can result in increasing the panic within the horse, elevating the danger significantly.

The anatomy of the horse is such that a grouping of nerves is placed directly over the heart and lungs, just under the skin. Mother Nature meant this to be a protective shield guarding attack against these vital organs. The canine family would be most likely to attack this area. When horses possess great sensitivity in this region, they are prone to quickly act out against intrusion.

An expert in equine anatomy would tell you that just under the girth there is spider-web-like grouping of nerves called a ganglion. Some horses have an extreme sensitivity connected to this ganglion, others a milder form. The first saddle of almost any horse will engender sensitivity to the fore-flank ganglion. Most will soon accept it, but some will become cinch-bound.

Question 127

My horse is very girthy ... she starts wiggling immediately when you bend down to get the cinch. When you tighten the girth she rears up and, if the rope breaks, she falls back. I am concerned she is going to hurt herself or me. I know it is from someone traumatizing her prior to me, but how do I fix it? I tried tightening the girth from other side and that worked for only one day.

Answer

The following is my recommendation for dealing with the condition already in place. With your horse in a loose box at least 12 feet (4 metres) square, put a substantial stable blanket on her and fasten all of the belts and buckles. Over the blanket, in the area of the heart, place an elastic over-girth. I prefer the type with a breast collar.

These over-girths can be purchased at a good tack shop and are generally about 4 inches (10 centimetres) in width and easily stretched by the human hand. Place the breast collar appropriately, and buckle up the elastic over-girth so it is just touching the skin. Allow your horse a few minutes in the loose box to become accustomed to the over-girth, and then tighten a notch or two so it begins to stretch the elastic material.

This girth is easily expandable and the horse usually does not react to it as violently as she would a less forgiving cinch or girth. You should continue to tighten periodically until you have stretched the girth sufficiently to snugly encircle the heart-girth area of the horse. It is appropriate to allow her to carry this apparatus around the loose box for up to three or four hours. Usually, within two or three days of this treatment, your horse will accept the elastic over-girth without a girthy response. When your horse is comfortable, you can go to the next step in the process.

It should be noted that it is never appropriate to girth or saddle a cinchy horse while it is tied. Your question is very frightening at that point where you describe the rope breaking. This response is extremely dangerous to both you and the horse. The skulls of many horses have been crushed as they break the tie, fall over backwards and strike the top of their head on the ground or floor. Necks can be broken, and the dorsal processes of the spine can also be injured or broken.

Once your horse can take the light, elastic girth relatively snug from the outset of the day, you can remove the blanket and allow the girth to come directly against her skin. Usually, this will not be of great concern to the horse. When this is accepted, initiate a pattern of putting the elastic girth on about half an hour before the time you intend to saddle your horse.

Most girthy horses will then take the girth quite comfortably if you tighten it gradually over a period of five to ten minutes. If your horse is more severely affected, simply extend the duration of each of these procedures until your horse is totally relaxed. Most girthy horses will be relatively free of this anxiety within a month or so if you are diligent about following these procedures to the letter.

One should be careful to always use a clean girth or cinch. I believe that it is an advantage to use the sheep-wool type. This can be a portable cover for the girth, or it can be the permanent type. Some of the artificial wool girths are just as effective as the authentic ones and are often easier to clean and care for. Wider girths are easier on the cinch-bound horse than narrow girths. If a horse acts out violently, this means that you have advanced the process too quickly. Make your transitions more gradual.

In dealing with a girthy horse, one should allow the horse to walk, trot and canter before mounting. As I am not a proponent of single-line lungeing, I would recommend long-lining your horse to achieve these gaits. Loose lungeing is also fine. This is much easier if you have a round pen, but that is not essential. A square pen is just fine, so long as the footing is acceptable for all three gaits. Mount only when your horse has comfortably given you all three gaits in a relaxed and cooperative manner.

Recommended additional resource: 7

HEAD-SHY HORSES AND TAKING THE BIT

Once more, these remedial problems have usually been created by past experiences and must be dealt with in a considerate and respectful manner. There is no forcing a horse to drop a head-shy condition or to accept the bit.

If a head-shy condition exists that has been caused by human mistreatment, then it is the horseperson's obligation to work with the animal in an effort to gain his trust. It is incumbent upon the human to create an environment where the horse repeatedly thinks he is going to have pain administered to the area of the head and then doesn't.

There are many elements to the recommendations that I make regarding head-shy horses. This section should be helpful to anyone who is experiencing difficulties with placing the bit in the horse's mouth or passing the crown of the bridle over the ears.

Question 128

My horse has difficulty taking the bit. It was recommended by someone that I use a bitless bridle for her, but I don't know how to use one and no one will help me. They will only help with a bit. My horse has never bitten, reared, bucked or been difficult in any way. She just gets very scared of the bit.

Answer

I sympathize with the problem you are having. Horses often come to me in the same condition you have outlined in your question. I will never understand how professional horsemen can feel that violence and brutality can solve the condition you have described. This behaviour is one of the few where I recommend a food substance.

I place honey first on a stick and ask the horse to take the stick in the mouth, licking the honey off. I then put honey on a bit with no bridle and repeat the process. Before long, the horse will follow me around and attempt to put the bit on himself. I have had good outcomes from this process.

Often horses become fearful when they hear the sound of metallic bits. In such cases Mylar or Happy Mouth bits are quite effective. These are made from a plastic-type substance that will take the honey quite well. The honey taste will remain on the soft mouthpiece, and you can put it on and take it off many times with your horse still experiencing the taste of the honey.

Note that it is quite possible to work without a bridle on the bit. It is easiest to work with the bit as a solo object, without reins either. Get in a mood to have fun with this. I recommend that you work with your horse in a box stall (loose box). If you put the horse's tail in a safe corner, then it is easier to approach the muzzle area. Don't be forceful with the honey-coated stick; start by putting it in the corner of the mouth and on to the tongue. Continue this work until you can pass it through the front teeth and on to the tongue so that the horse tastes the honey.

Experience is always valuable in these areas. I would like you to realize that with my decades of work with horses I can take the most difficult sort and cause him to reach out consciously to take the bit in two or three sessions of forty-five minutes to one hour. When you can achieve this level of acceptance from your horse, it is fun. When it is fun, it happens faster and more effectively.

Wherever a bitless bridle can be advantageous to the horse owner, I recommend using the Dually halter. It can serve as a normal halter and is invaluable for educating the horse in many areas covered by answers in this book. It comes complete with its own DVD to help you in learning to use it.

Recommended additional resources: 1, 5

Question 129

We are starting a two-year-old filly, and putting a bridle on her and taking it off is virtually impossible. Can you tell us how we can overcome her dislike of the bridle going over her ears?

Answer

I would estimate that 90 per cent of head-shy horses are man-made, as a result of people striking the horse's head with ropes or whips or 'twitching' an ear (a procedure whereby a rope is twisted around the ear to produce pain, forcing the horse to comply with a person's demand). The memory of this can easily cause a horse to be reticent about allowing touch in that area. It is also important, however, to acknowledge those 10 per cent of horses that are head-shy without the intervention of a human. In these cases, physical discomfort of some type is the cause, and it is imperative to have your horse checked for lice, ticks or other parasites, as well as dental problems, before you start to re-train the behaviour.

Trust is the key to enabling your filly to relax while you handle her ears. Trust is the key to everything I do around horses. The first step is always using Join-Up to build and repair trust using the horse's language *Equus*. Then you should start handling her head, using advance and retreat. If at all possible, use the Dually halter so you can train your filly to yield to pressure on her head instead of flinging her head up into the pressure.

It is important that when the filly momentarily accepts the feeling of your hands around the sensitive areas on her head, you walk away instantly, thus releasing the pressure on her. Once you and your filly are comfortable and relaxed with this process, you can move on to introducing a hairdryer to her. Spray her with water so she is wet over her head and neck, and have a handler hold her so you can operate the dryer.

Holding the hairdryer away from your filly, gradually move the flow of air over her hindquarters and up to the shoulder, beginning to condition her to the flow of air and the sound of the motor. Start to move the flow of air over her head and ears, using advance and retreat methods until she begins to accept the stimulus. Once she is comfortable with the air blowing directly on her ears, you can start to use your hand on and around her ears, and introduce a brush, clippers etc.

Please find and read a copy of my textbook, if possible, as this book outlines the process in far greater detail, with diagrams and photos to assist your learning. You can also attend training programmes to help your filly re-learn the appropriate behaviour.

Recommended additional resources: 1, 7, 15

THE ROUND PEN

This is my office, my workshop and my home away from home. It is an extremely helpful piece of equipment and I recommend that every horseperson gain access to one. A round enclosure simply creates an environment where there are no corners. A square or rectangular enclosure tends to allow the horse to lose energy by becoming psychologically trapped in a corner.

The round pen encourages a free and continuous flow of energy, without any interruption at least from the structure itself. For a broad middle category of sizes of the horse, I recommend a fifty-foot (sixteen-metre) diameter. This will allow for comfortable cantering with correct use of the leads.

Should one already have a conventional enclosure (with corners) approximately this size, it can be easily adapted by panelling off the corners. This creates an octagon, which is a near approximation to a round enclosure. While it is second best, I have often worked in an octagon pen and found it to be quite acceptable.

Question 130

I was just wondering if you have to use an enclosed area for Join-Up, as I live on a Scottish island, and it is hard to get access to one. Would a small field do?

Answer

The book *Shy Boy: The Horse That Came in from the Wild* and the documentaries made about Shy Boy depict how I did Join-Up with him with virtually no enclosure whatsoever. The fact is that it was nearly twelve miles to the nearest fence when I was causing him to Join-Up with me. I suppose it is a possibility that your Scottish island is even smaller than the 42,000 acres where I worked with Shy Boy!

Every time you approach your horse in the field, the stable or the round pen, you are communicating in the language *Equus*. The way you hold your body, the placement of your eyes and the movement of your hands all tell the horse your thoughts and intentions. It is important to remember that communication with your horse is a continuous process. As long as you have a safe environment, Join-Up is possible. If you have a large field in which to do Join-Up, you may need to walk a little bit further than if you were in a round pen, but you will be amazed to see the horse begin to move in circles and arcs around you as it communicates.

However, please do not lose sight of the fact that a safe, round enclosure, approximately fifty feet (sixteen metres) in diameter with good footing, is the optimum environment in which to do Join-Up. I answer this question all over the world, and I understand the fact that people want to know if they can do the work without a round pen. The answer is yes, but a major part of the answer is that an appropriate round pen is the best way to go.

Many horsepeople further inquire as to what the recommended design is for the optimum round pen, so I will give here a brief outline of what I consider to be the best design.

Round pens have been constructed of many different materials: logs, planks, stones or even tyres. In recent years, I have seen many round pens made of solar tape. People actually tell me that once a horse is trained to the electrical tape, this works just fine.

History shows that round pens, which were originally used as a part of traditional training, have varied in size over the centuries. The methods used were often brutal and many of these structures had a solid post in the centre to restrain untrained horses. I have seen sizes varying between 30 feet (10 metres) and 150 feet (50 metres) in diameter. On my farm, Flag Is Up, I built my round pens with solid plank walls approximately 8 feet high. They are 50 feet (16 metres) in diameter. I consider this the optimum size for normal saddle horses of fourteen to seventeen hands.

The factor I observe most closely in determining pen size is the capability of the horses I am working to canter maintaining the same lead, front and rear. Very big Warmbloods may require a slightly larger diameter in order to move in a coordinated manner. For the smaller breeds, the diameter can actually come down to about forty-six feet with no problem.

One of the most critical aspects of a round pen is the footing, which is important both for the safety and the performance of the horse. Any accepted horse-show style of soil or artificial surface is acceptable, so long as it offers good traction as well as good cushioning. While my walls slope slightly outward at the top, I have learned that this is not a necessity to clear the legs of the rider. A wall straight up and down will do just fine.

On my travels around the world in recent years, I have worked with portable round pens. They are made of welded mesh wire so that people can see what I am doing and the fence is straight up and down. I have dealt with more than seven thousand horses for public audiences and whether or not it's just luck, all these horses have remained physically sound through the process.

It is a good idea to place the round pen in an area as free of distractions as possible. Horses will respond to educational sessions far better when not disturbed by the sight of other horses, people, animals or other activities. A hedge around the round pen can often assist in this effort.

Recommended additional resource: 10

EQUIPMENT

Every question-and-answer session seems to include a few inquiries about the equipment I use. It will serve every horseperson well to remember that the most important part of any piece of equipment is the hands that hold it.

All horsemen should seek to use the best equipment possible, while at the same time never allowing the equipment to become a substitute for good horsemanship. Someone once told me that, while a good carpenter will always out-perform a bad carpenter, it is likely that you will see the best equipment in the toolbox of the good carpenter.

If this sounds like a chicken-and-egg situation, then I think that the good horseperson should always come first; and then that individual should set out to be equipped in the best possible way. We owe it to our horses and to ourselves as well to make our work as easy as possible, because that tends to increase our competence.

Question 131

Why do you do your Join-Up demonstrations using an English saddle and never a Western? Is that why lots of cowboys think Join-Up is for dressage queens?

Answer

There are many reasons why the saddle that I choose to use for my demonstrations has evolved to its present form. It is not an English saddle. It is not a military saddle. It is not a Western saddle. It is a modified exercise saddle of the kind used on most Thoroughbred racehorses for morning workouts.

The saddle I have chosen has practically no tree at all. As you might imagine, as I travel the world doing my demonstrations, I deal with horses of all sizes and shapes. If I had a full tree in a saddle, it would be virtually impossible to cause it to fit the wide array of horses that I work with.

I buy these exercise saddles from a company that provides them for the racing industry. Once the saddle is in my possession, I then take it to one of the saddlers who have been trained to make the modifications I have designed. The first thing they do is to replace the billet straps (those straps that the girth connects to on each side of the saddle). They attach billets about three times the length of the original ones. This allows me to use a very short girth, which will fit a tiny horse or a pony when it's taken up to the top on both sides. If the girth is attached to the longest notches, then it will fit even a big draught horse.

I use a soft girth with elastic on the offside connection. While the saddler is replacing the billets, he builds into the front of the saddle a special handhold similar to the one you might see on a bareback bronc rigging. This allows my riders to remain in the saddle even through sessions of bucking.

D-rings are attached in three strategic locations. One is at the extreme rear portion of the saddle. Two more are placed in the front of the saddle about 8 inches or so from the pommel. The rear one is part of the attachment for the mannequin rider that I use for horses that want to buck. The two in front will allow me to attach a breast collar so that the saddle can't slide back.

It is true that my riders can feel the horse and use leg aids that are more difficult to achieve with a Western saddle, but the primary reason why I use this type of saddle is that it is light in weight. If I travelled the world with a Western saddle, the airlines would be levying thousands of dollars of overweight charges. The inconvenience of the size would also be a factor. And, as I have already mentioned, fitting all the horses I deal with would be virtually impossible.

To answer the question in full, please let me assure you that the dressage people of the world ask me why I don't use a dressage saddle, while the Western people inquire why I don't have my riders use that sort of equipment. It has nothing to do with dressage, Western or English. It is a saddle that has been especially adapted to dealing with horses being started or remedial horses across the spectrum of size, breed and discipline.

Question 132

Do you recommend martingales, tie-downs, draw reins or chambons?

Answer

I would like you to think about this one carefully. I am being asked here for an opinion on equipment that is fully extrinsic, issuing demand through harsh pressure. I believe that a horse properly trained by my methods virtually never needs any one of these aids. If I were asked if I have ever found them to be helpful, I would have to answer honestly that at one time or another, I have found all of them helpful. It is difficult ever to say never, but the need for harsh equipment is extremely rare when dealing with horses trained by my methods.

Having expressed my own position, I would like to now give you more information in an attempt to educate readers in the potential uses of these pieces of equipment, each of them unique. I would like my students to regard each of the identified objects as items to assist, as opposed to items with which to train.

The martingale is a piece of equipment that exists in several forms: there is a standing martingale, a running martingale, a French martingale and a German martingale, each of which is used in the mainstream of horsemanship worldwide. If one were to investigate, I bet one would find there was a Russian version, and even one used in Mongolia. For the purpose of this answer, I will deal with a more generic mixture of the mainstream martingales.

The running martingale is typically used on Western and (off the track) racehorses and in the UK on virtually all ponies, riding horses and show jumpers. I realize that many other disciplines in the USA embrace the running martingale, but the two I have mentioned use it more often than the others. It is a shoulder yoke with a ring in the centre of the chest. It circles the base of the neck and attaches to the girth at the bottom, passing between the front legs. There are generally two strips of leather about one foot long with a ring on the end of each of them. They are attached to the chest ring of the shoulder yoke.

Each rein is passed through one of the two rings and then up to the rider's hands. If the horse attempts to raise his head above the natural level, the martingale comes into play to assist the rider in maintaining a reasonable head position. This means that the horse is restricted, and therefore the martingale is extrinsic. Obviously it would be better if we could cause the horse to want to keep his head low, but sometimes the martingale will help us for a while, and then we can remove it when our horse is a bit easier to work with.

The standing martingale (tie-down) is used most often with driving horses and rodeo horses. It has the same yoke as the running martingale, but then only one spoke off the chest ring directly to a cavesson (noseband). It is adjusted so that the length of leather tightens when the horse raises his head above the desired level. It is absolute; there is no flexibility.

A rope horse will use the tie-down to lean against as he stops, taking the pull of a heavy animal on the end of the rope. Most ropers feel that the horse is more comfortable with this support, and their performance is far more predictable than without it. Those involved with heavy draft horses which pull sizable vehicles or implements will say that their horses use the standing martingale as a support during stressful tugging. I do not feel that the standing martingale has much value in disciplines outside these two uses.

The French and German martingales differ again in that they are generally only used to tie the two reins together just behind the bit. They simply exercise a steadying effect. While many European horsemen insist that they are effective, I tend to find little value in them and have never used them in my own training programmes.

Draw reins are typically made from two extra-long pieces of leather that are used as reins. Please try to picture the rider sitting in the saddle with two strips of leather buckled together at the hands. Further, picture that each strip of leather has its own side of the horse to operate on, one on the left and one on the right. We will call these two strips 'reins'. Next, take each rein and pass it through a ring on the bit and then to the girth on its respective side.

When the rider applies pressure to these reins on either side or both, the horse's muzzle is required to come closer to his chest. There is no question this mechanism is extrinsic (it demands), but in the early stages of some training it can be helpful to assist in the creation of a desirable head position without a great deal of effort on the part of the rider. I do not advocate its use, but rather recommend that more time be spent encouraging this head position with good horsemanship rather than extrinsic equipment. There is no substitute for the use of experienced hands to create a desirable head position.

Chambons are often made in ultra-complicated fashions. They vary greatly with the area and the horseperson involved. It is my opinion that they can be extremely helpful for a horse that tends to hollow out its back and travel with head and tail high and the centre of the spine low. This is an undesirable position, as it tends to create many forms of back and pelvis problems.

Nelson Pessoa, one of the world's leading trainers in the discipline of show jumping, has created a form of chambon that he calls 'The Pessoa'. It is used specifically without a rider, so that one can lunge the horse without suffering many of the bad effects of single-line lungeing. It lowers the head and rounds the back. I recommend chambons, but only for training on long lines, not for riding.

Question 133

I am having a difficult time deciding what bit to use on my horse. Why would you recommend your bit over the typical ones I find on the market? And how do the various sizes affect my horse and me?

Answer

I have designed my bit to be made of black iron; it rusts. Bits that don't rust are most often made of stainless steel. They look nice, are easy to clean and last well because they are simply harder and more durable given that they spend a lot of time in a moist environment and also being chewed on by the horse's teeth.

I personally remember stainless steel coming to popularity right after the Second World War; the bit-makers referred to it as Monel steel. I thought it was wonderful as I often had the assignment to clean the bits. It seemed like a logical way to have a shiny, attractive bit that looked clean and lasted a long time. The problem with this theory is that nobody checked with the horses.

By some time around 1960, I heard the top trainers suggesting that their horses seemed to be happier with the old, rusty, black iron bits. I found myself digging out some of the older bits and re-acquainting myself with the behaviour of my horses, comparing how they reacted to the shiny bits and to the rusty ones. Lo and behold, I concluded that these trainers were right. The horses much preferred the old-style black iron. Virtually every trainer agrees that the presence of some copper in the mouth creates more natural moisture, thus presenting the horse with a situation whereby the bit sits much more comfortably on lubricated tissue than if his mouth was dry.

You might ask: Why not make the whole mouthpiece copper? In fact, some companies have done just that. A pure copper mouthpiece, however, is very soft and not sufficiently durable. Horses will literally chew a pure copper mouthpiece, often creating an unusable bit in just a few months. Still, the top racehorse trainer D. Wayne Lucas prefers pure copper mouthpieces and simply throws them away every six months or so.

I have designed my bit so that it is made of the metallic combination I feel addresses the issues most effectively: that is, black iron as a principal metal, with copper inlaid in strips so that it is protected from chewing by the stronger black iron. The presence of the copper creates the desired moisture. To address the look of the bit, I designed it so that the portions outside the horse's mouth are stainless steel, nice and shiny with the look people desire.

The portion of the bit just outside the lips is designed so that it is not simply a ring passing through the mouthpiece, but a barrel-shaped tube, which is far more comfortable when guiding the horse left or right. The name of this particular arrangement is 'modified egg butt'; some might call it a 'modified D-ring'. I believe that I have created a bit that has the overall look of a professional piece of equipment while being comfortable and acceptable for the horse, as we so desperately need it to be if we are going to be successful trainers.

I am not a fan of thin-gauged mouthpieces. They are far more severe than a large gauge when pressure is applied by the reins. By its very nature, the snaffle bit rises off the tongue when contact occurs. As the centre portion of the mouthpiece rises, the contact points become the sublingual bars of the horse's mouth (gums), which travel on both the left and right sides of the horse's mouth just at the margins.

Horses fortunately have a gap in their dental structure right where we want the bit to go. The bars constitute those areas of the gums, which are free of teeth. When the bit makes contact with those bars, the size of the mouthpiece itself is critical. A tiny, wire-like mouthpiece would tend to cut in, and repeated scarring creates a hard-mouthed horse.

The protection of the precious soft tissue of the horse's mouth is critical to the overall performance of the horse, no matter what discipline you intend to follow. We all want a horse with a sensitive mouth, but we are responsible for creating that sensitivity or destroying it. The bit is our partner in that effort.

Because my work is global, I must address the particular issues raised by extra large Warmbloods and also the tiny heads of the Arabs I work with. I have designed my bits with a thick- and a thin-gauged mouthpiece. The thick mouthpiece is naturally heavier and more appropriate for the large breeds. Conversely, the thin should be used on sensitive Arabians, Quarter Horses and the lighter breeds. My thick mouthpiece is simply too large for the smaller mouths. It is about four times the thickness of what is considered a normal snaffle by today's standards. My smaller mouthpiece is more appropriate for the lighter breeds, but it should be understood that it is still double the size of today's typical snaffle, therefore kinder by far to these sensitive mouths. The length of the mouthpiece itself is longer or shorter to accommodate the width of the mouth on the various sizes of the horses in question. The owner of an Arabian horse will obviously want the 5-inch bit, while the owner of a show jumper will generally be looking at the 5½-inch.

I often refer to one particular anecdote when discussing black iron as a preferred metal for bits. The largest snaffle bit competition in the world is the National Reined Cowhorse Association Snaffle Bit Futurity. It took approximately twenty years for all the contestants to come round to the idea of using black iron. In 2004, about three hundred contestants turned up for the competition. Every competitor had a black iron mouthpiece.

Question 134

Please tell me about your long lines. How long are they? What are they made of and why do you recommend them?

Answer

My long lines are very important to me. They assist me with the training of the horses, but I have designed them so that they are safe for my hands. Prior to 1996, I bought commercial long lines that were available in the tack shops.

In Dallas, Texas, in 1996, I had a situation where a horse became very frightened because of a loud noise in my audience. He blasted across the round pen strictly out of fear. I was feeding one of these light, flimsy lines when it flipped a half hitch around my little finger. The horse hit the end of the line giving me a fierce jolt. He then stopped, and I approached him.

As I walked up to the horse, I noticed that there was blood on my trousers. I looked down to see that the end of my little finger on my left hand was hanging on a thread of skin. I announced that if there was a doctor in the audience, I would appreciate it if he would come and meet me when I had finished working with this horse.

Sticking the end of the little finger between two others, I put my rider on and completed my work with this horse. Immediately afterwards I met the doctor, and after some argument he agreed to tape the finger back on so I could do the next and last horse, after which I would go straight to the hospital to see if they could put it back on again.

He was a hand surgeon. Can you imagine being so lucky as to have a hand surgeon in your audience at a time like that? I made my appointment, he sewed the finger-end back on, and it's there today. Not much to brag about, I will admit – it has no feeling and no nail; but at least it's still a part of me.

Immediately after that event, my son and I went on a worldwide hunt for the right material to use in designing the perfect driving line. My lines are 30 feet long and slightly weighted in the last three feet by being doubled in thickness. It makes them easier to cast. They are covered in a soft blend material and cushion-filled with cotton to keep them plump and less likely to whip into those half hitches.

These lines come in pairs and each has a high-quality brass clip on it. I use them for years before they need to be replaced, and I haven't had a hand injury since I created the particular design I have described.

Question 135

My horse bobs his head when I ask him to tuck or collect his stride. Can you explain this?

Answer

Virtually every time a horse 'misbehaves' from the standpoint of head carriage, it is caused by the rider's hands. Whether we realize it or not, horses can only react to our signals; they just don't act without cause. I suggest the following mouthing procedure be employed.

I have found the use of side reins to be the most effective treatment for the behaviour you describe. Attach a pair of elastic and leather side reins to a surcingle and allow the horse to toss his head, simply meeting the side reins and stretching the elastics. Normally, horses will stop the head tossing after four or five sessions following these recommendations. I have used this method of mouthing a horse for well over fifty years now and have found it to be the most effective.

One should be mindful of the need gradually to tighten the side reins so that slightly more pressure is applied as you work through these exercises. It is helpful for one to long-line while the side reins are in place, as this action more closely approximates the act of riding the horse. If this causes the head bobbing described, that's wonderful,

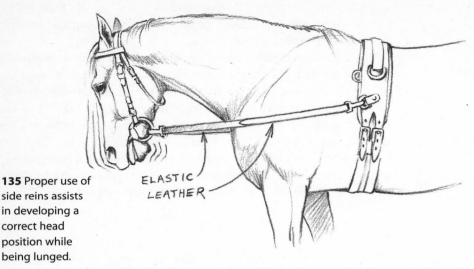

135 Proper use of side reins assists in developing a correct head position while being lunged.

ELASTIC LEATHER

as it allows the horse to learn while activating the elastics in the side reins.

It is important to be patient and make changes very gradually. A change made too abruptly can cause a horse to fight the side reins and might even result in its falling over. Err on the side of caution, but once you have cooperation, then it is fine to increase the tension.

Recommended additional resource: 1

Question 136

I have a horse that kicks in the trailer while travelling. He also kicks the wall once in a while in the stable. What can you tell me about the use of kicking rings?

Answer

The kicking ring is a device commonly used to discourage and preferably stop a horse from the annoying and potentially dangerous habit of kicking. This habit can inflict injury, not only to the animal itself, but also to other animals, people and structures in the vicinity.

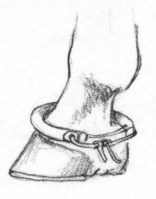

136.1 View of each side of kicking ring.

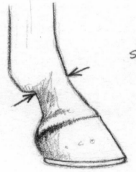

SIZE THE RING TO FIT THE NARROWEST PART OF THE PASTERN.

The actual ring is simply a smooth, round steel bar, ⅝ inch in diameter, bent into a 'bracelet' shape. You or your farrier easily can create a set – just be extremely careful that all rough edges have been smoothed off to prevent any chafing.

Construct the ring at an appropriate size to slip on the horse's upper pastern area. It will be held in place as it slides down to the wider area above the coronary band. This device does not inflict pain, only minor discomfort, which distracts the horse from whatever it is that makes him think he wants to kick.

136.2 The drawing shows how the ring becomes uncomfortable when the horse kicks.

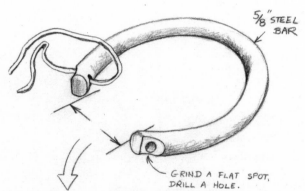

5/8" STEEL BAR

GRIND A FLAT SPOT, DRILL A HOLE.

136.3 The leather thong keeps the ring secure.

The side benefit is that the massaging of the coronary band as the horse walks around stimulates healthy hoof growth!

Recommended additional resource: 1

In gathering the material for this book, I found dozens of questions that raised the issue of whether or not bits are necessary in the process of riding and training horses. To cover this subject, I have chosen the following question.

Question 137

Are horse bits absolutely necessary? Is it not possible to use a Dually halter to ride with?

Answer

It is absolutely appropriate to ride in a Dually halter. Once you have tried it, you will see many reasons why it is an effective piece of equipment with which to ride, lead and train your horse. In the world of horsemanship there is a piece of equipment called a side pull. Many horsemen recommend it. The Dually is simply a modified side pull.

The two training rings provide a natural attachment for each of the reins. While you use both reins for riding or long lining, I recommend the use of one rein while schooling from the ground. The Dually halter comes with its own DVD to assist you in the process of learning how to use it.

Recommended additional resource: 5

Question 138

How do I get my horse to stand still? He often fidgets in a line-up when I am in a competition. If I am riding out with friends and we decide to stop, he is a real pain because he keeps twisting and turning. No matter what I do, he will not stand still.

Answer

It is extremely important for all horsepeople to imprint a value of standing still within the minds of their horses. Standing still is one of the most important things that we can teach our horses. Until they find value in standing motionless, it is very difficult to cause them to be patient with the farrier, the veterinarian or even the person trying to mount.

This answer will be as comprehensive as I can make it so as to cover the long list of important reasons why it is critical to teach a horse to stand still. Standing to be mounted might represent the most important lesson our horses can learn from the standpoint of the safety of the rider. Injuries to people while mounting are at the top of the list where serious accidents are concerned.

Mounting is a time when the human is at a distinct disadvantage. They are off balance and in a position that is awkward to say the least. People who are not in the best physical condition are even more vulnerable at this time than those who are physically fit. Even the fit ones, however, face danger whenever they are in the process of mounting.

It is imperative that horses stand motionless while people go through the process of getting from the ground to the saddle. Anything short of this can produce an accident, which might be very minor or extremely serious. A man was killed recently in our community while mounting his horse.

A client of mine who has ridden for more than thirty years was recently injured while mounting his horse in the aisle-way of his stable. He told me that the horse moved just a little as his right leg was going over the top, causing him to squeeze with his right leg before he was fully in the saddle. His leg pressed into the horse's off-flank (right flank); at this, the horse bolted with my client hanging on the side. He hit his shoulder on the stable and was thrown from the saddle, badly bruising a knee. His head was banged at some point, producing a concussion, and the combination of these injuries had him in hospital for several days.

He was laughing about it when he told me the story, but it could have been much worse. As you can well imagine, his head might have struck a solid object as the horse moved quickly in fright.

Standing in the show-ring line-up is the least of our troubles, but the rest of your question gives me the opportunity to address the much broader concern, which is training the horse to find value in standing still. It doesn't matter whether it's for the veterinarian, the farrier or a rider mounting, remaining motionless is a part of reasonable ground manners for every horse. The Dually halter is the definitive piece of equipment called for in this case. In my concepts, it is critical to have and fully understand the use of the Dually halter.

The Dually halter is designed so that it gets smaller when the horse resists it and bigger and more comfortable when the horse cooperates. With this principle in mind, watch the DVD that comes with the Dually and introduce yourself to the correct way to use it. I recommend that one first practise using the Dually halter with trained horses, and then progress to the more difficult ones.

As always, I recommend that you first do a good Join-Up with your horse and then that you school your horse to the Dually halter following the recommendations on the DVD. Once your horse is cooperative with the halter, then you can begin the lessons necessary to cause your horse to learn the value of standing still.

At the outset, the process of training the horse to stand still is executed by working from the ground. Stop your horse in a safe location (that is, where there is good footing and no dangerous circumstances in the environment) and step back away from him, leaving a bit of slack in the lead. I use a thirty-foot (ten-metre) driving line, and I recommend a minimum length of twenty feet (six metres).

Stand simply looking at your horse, and when he moves any foot school him with the Dually halter. This means tightening the line and using the halter to guide the horse firmly back to the spot where you originally placed him. Repeat this process until your horse stands for twenty to thirty seconds without moving a foot.

Having accomplished this goal, step forward, give your horse a rub between the eyes and lead him around in a circle, allowing his muscles to relax. Then place your horse on another safe spot and repeat the process. You can begin to build on the requirements so that in time the horse will stand for three, four or five minutes remaining completely motionless.

Making the transition to standing still under saddle is done by using a bitless bridle, if you have one. This will ensure the safety of your horse's mouth. Sitting on the horse, use the bitless bridle just as the Dually halter, causing your horse to be less than comfortable when he moves a foot. It is best to rein back during the schooling process.

If one is diligent about using the recommended equipment and executing the desired techniques, it is possible to train a horse to stand for very long period of time without changing the position of one foot. Be careful not to require the horse to stand motionless to the extent that he becomes extremely uncomfortable due to cramping muscles. Be fair with your horse and he will be fair with you.

Recommended additional resources: 1, 3, 5

Question 139

My horse refuses to accept a turnout rug. I have been kicked several times and my hands have been burned because the horse bolts away from me as I attempt to put the rug over the body. He has pulled back and broken the tie several times. Please help me!

Answer

This problem exists worldwide. I am sure that many horse owners endure the behaviour you have outlined without seeking assistance. I am pleased that you have reached out to solve your horse's problem as it may well help many other owners.

Obviously, I myself have experienced spooky behaviour from horses as I have attempted to put the first rug on them. I well remember An Act, whom I bought in Kentucky and transported to California. I recall the moment when I tried to rig him up for the first time after his arrival at Flag Is Up Farms. He was in his loose box, and when he exploded at the sight of the rug coming over him, I genuinely thought I was going to be killed.

Before I go into the body of this answer, I feel I should be clear that I recommend one never place the first rug on a horse that is tied up. It is also true that one should never tie up a horse for rugging if there is any anticipation of trouble at all. If one discovers a fear of the rug, then there should be no attempt to rug up until there is a certainty that all fear is alleviated.

It is my recommendation that you carry out all of the procedures that I recommend for the spooky horse. This will include Join-Up, training to the Dually halter, plastic bags on a stick and even a large tarpaulin. Once you are proficient in applying my concepts regarding spooky horses, then I advise you to repeat these processes until it is possible to cover the horse in a plastic tarpaulin without evoking spooky behaviour.

During my demonstrations, I often find it possible to reach a point where I can cover the horse with a tarpaulin about ten feet (approximately three metres) square. I can normally lead the horse around, allowing the tarpaulin to move about, without great consternation on the part of the horse. It is not necessary for this to be accomplished in less than half an hour, but I suggest that anyone reasonably familiar with proper handling of horses can get it done in two or three half-hour sessions.

Many times when I suggest this to inquiring owners, they return to say it didn't work for them. With further discussion, I come to find out that the methods they used bore very little resemblance to the ones I suggested. I can only be responsible for the methods that work for me, and they are certainly available; but they must be learned thoroughly and applied diligently.

The Dually halter should be used to educate the horse to cooperate with the halter rather than resist it. This process is fully demonstrated on the DVD that accompanies the Dually halter. With regard to the use of the plastic bags, they should be presented to the horse in such a fashion that he learns to relax, which causes them to go away. This should be repeated until several plastic shopping bags fixed to the end of a bamboo cane can be rapidly moved towards the horse, stroking his body and legs and even up between the hind legs.

When the subject horse will allow the plastic bags to fly all about him and touch him over his entire anatomy, then one is ready to move on to the plastic tarpaulin. It can be rubbed over the horse at first, and even spread out on the ground to walk over. The Dually halter will greatly assist with cooperation during this process. At that point, one can begin to place the tarpaulin over the horse, first rolled up to reduce the stimulus and eventually wide open and tossed over the horse, the same as one would do with a rug.

Recommended additional resources: 1, 5, 7, 14

Question 140

I attended one of your demonstrations recently and was anxious to learn every detail of your work. I sailed boats as a kid, and I heard you mention a few knots that you said were useful. Can you please tell me which ones you use and why?

Answer

Knots are a subject that I often visit during the course of one of my demonstrations. I believe it is essential that every horseperson has a good working knowledge of the essential half-dozen or so knots that are most often used when working with horses.

The bowline is a knot that, in my opinion, anyone calling himself a horseman absolutely must understand. It is a knot that can be tied around the horse's neck: no matter how hard they pull, it won't allow the rope to get tighter. Thus it is virtually impossible for a horse to choke himself with the bowline knot.

It is also true that no matter how much pressure is applied to the rope, the bowline – unlike many knots – will remain in such a state that it is easy to untie. One can put a bowline knot in a rope, tow a truck with it and then just pop it loose very easily.

In the world of tying horses up, there are several slipknots that can be employed. One will tighten up on the post and another won't. Some are easier to untie if a horse is in trouble and some are more difficult. One should become familiar with two or three of the best slipknots to use when tying a horse to a post, tree or hitch rack.

The clove hitch is a knot that has several forms and applications. It has many uses in the horse industry, and one should become familiar with it. The clove hitch can be used in combination with various slipknots. It is the type of knot that would keep a rope from sliding down a sleek pole that a horse is tied to.

In sailing, one must become familiar with dozens of knots. It doesn't seem too much to ask that horsemen become familiar with the variations of three knots, whose use will dramatically improve the safety of both people and horses. The knowledge of the bowline, the slipknot and the clove hitch is essential for every horseperson.

Question 141

I have heard you discuss carrying a good pocketknife while working around horses. Can you elaborate?

Answer

Knife makers have recently designed a knife that is perfect for the horseman. They tell me it was designed for professional fishermen. It is made of a type of steel that does not corrode and is equipped with a clip on it so that it sits at the top of your pocket, easily reachable. There are features about it that allow one to open the knife with one hand.

I suggest that every horseperson should have one, and that they should keep it in the same place all the time. One should practise removing it from the pocket and opening it with one hand. This should become a muscle memory act, which can be done over and over without mishandling.

The knife that I use is only about 4 inches (10 centimetres) long, so it easily fits into the pocket of my jeans. The blade has a ring on the back portion of it, which allows me to grip it with my thumb and index finger. With a learned flick of the wrist I can open the knife and have it in a position to use within a couple of seconds.

STABLE VICES AND BOREDOM

This is a topic that is becoming more important as our world grows smaller. Horses are kept in confinement and not allowed on the free, open ranges for which nature has conditioned them. People have become busier in this last century, with less time for the horses in their care.

These facts come to create a situation for our horses that significantly encourages boredom. Once boredom sets in, then stable vices increase. I must be careful not to suggest that busy people should not have a horse. I want everybody that desires to have a horse in his or her life to have one.

It is my obligation to assist where I can in helping busy people with ideas for creating a reasonable existence for our equine partners. There are many ways to address the issues of small spaces and busy schedules. We just have to be ever diligent in exploring all the options.

Question 142

My horse is bored in the stable. How can I solve this? Are there tricks or toys for horses that have to stay in a stable many hours a day?

Answer

There are many tricks and toys available to you these days. As I visit the racetracks of the world I come in contact with horses that are often stabled up to twenty-three hours per day. Obviously stable vices are exhibited by these horses more than those in virtually any other discipline.

Hay nets are often used to encourage the horse to graze throughout the day and evening. These hay nets will be hung just outside the door opening, and the horses are allowed to reach out of their stalls with their heads. Since the door opening at typical tracks is closed only by a stall webbing about two feet wide and waist high, the horse can reach under them with the forelegs. This requires that the hay net be kept quite high so as to prevent horses from tangling their feet in them. I advocate feeding horses low, as their anatomy is constructed with that in mind. Hay nets, however, preclude that possibility leaving me less than enthusiastic about their use. I would only recommend them if they were very effective to alleviate boredom.

Many other objects are used in efforts to entertain the horse during the long hours in the stable. Tetherballs are often seen at the racetracks. Sometimes a horse will have three or four of them hanging in different locations so that he can swing them with his nose in a game-like fashion. Large beach balls rolling loose in the stall do the trick for some horses.

And then there are those horses that prefer animal friends. Goats and sheep are the animals most often used as horse playmates. I even saw a horse that had a pet parrot living in a cage just outside his door. The horse was terribly unhappy when the parrot was not there and clearly found him to be a valuable antidote to the boredom of this stable bound horse.

Music, and even certain grooms who are around a lot for a horse, can make a huge difference in the tranquillity of these animals. It is clear that a horse that is comfortable with his surroundings eats and performs better than a horse that lives in an anxious state. Observe your horses closely and try to see to their needs.

Question 143

I have a seven-year-old Quarter Horse gelding that is a cribber. What should I do to get him to stop this? And second, will the other horses in my barn learn this bad habit from him?

Answer

Cribbing, or crib-biting, is also called wind-sucking and a few other colloquial names. It is a habit generally thought to be motivated by boredom. I have never seen a mustang in the wild cribbing. Many of the old books will classify cribbing as a stable vice. This seems to be valid, since it generally occurs where horses are kept in small confined spaces.

A cure for cribbing has been sought for many decades. There are stories about trainers who used rather harsh techniques in an attempt to correct the habit of cribbing through training. I have never heard of the discovery of a successful system of training any horse not to crib. I believe that once the habit begins, it is with the horse for life.

In recent years, certain veterinary colleges have studied and perfected a surgical technique that has been effective in about 85 per cent of the cases treated. I have personally seen many horses that were corrected through this surgery and found that they were unable to collapse the pharynx and gulp air into the stomach.

The University of Kentucky did an experiment in the 1960s and 1970s on whether or not one horse could learn to crib from another. As I recall, their findings suggest that there is some learned habituation from one horse to another.

BUCKING

We will not successfully deal with all of the answers to this dangerous remedial problem by reading a single question and answer. The problem here is that while I get hundreds of questions about bucking, almost every one is the same and it goes like this, 'I have a horse and he bucks. What do I do?' I do not wish to throw out the section because there is only one question; it is too important. It is, however, my hope that this section will open minds to the need for better understanding of this dangerous activity.

While bucking is not the remedial act most likely to produce serious injury to humans, it is second only to refusing to stand for mounting. This places it in the extreme classification as a potential for danger. Unless a horse is a professional in rodeos, bucking is never OK.

Before starting work to address the issue of bucking, it is critically important to be sure that the anatomy of the horse is fully normal and free of pain. In addition, it is essential that the saddle, saddle pad and girth arrangements fit well and are appropriate for the anatomy of the horse in question.

Much of my life was spent with people who would advocate whipping the horse while bucking. They would suggest that this would teach the horse not to buck. I have concluded after decades of work that whipping the horse while bucking causes harder bucking and bucking more often.

Question 144

Why does my horse only buck in September? He is fine all year long, totally safe and a wonderful ride. In September, however, he bucks with me and has bucked me off two times now. I live near Munich, in Germany. Please help me.

Answer

When this question came through to me, I was on my signing stand at a Munich demonstration. I was immediately interested in what in the world could cause a horse to buck only in the month of September. I called for the owner please to come to the signing stand as I had questions I simply had to ask before I could answer this question with any degree of accuracy.

In about five minutes, a gentleman I would guess to be in his late forties approached my signing stand. He spoke no English, so we were communicating through my interpreter Ras Barthel. I inquired why he felt this horse bucked only in September. He said he had no idea. I asked him how often he rode his horse, and he said two to three times a week. I then confirmed with him that the horse was perfectly fine for eleven months out of the year, but then bucked like heck in September.

I asked what activity he engaged in with his horse. He told me that he was an ardent trail rider. He said that he loved to ride out in the woods, and that near his home in the Munich area there were many natural trails for him and his horse to enjoy along with two or three friends that he often rode with. My mind then headed in the direction of what equipment he used, and he explained that he rode in a typical English saddle of a show-jumping design. Then I inquired whether he rode in exactly the same place in September as he did in the other eleven months. When I asked this question I could see a light go on in his head.

'No,' he told Ras, 'in September I take my horse into the mountains about fifty miles from my home.' He went on to say that he had a cabin there and that he loved to go stag hunting in the month of September. I've no idea why I thought he might use a different saddle, but I asked him about that. He answered that when he went hunting he used an American-style Western saddle.

Now a light went on in *my* head! I asked if it had two girths or just one. His response was that it had two, and I needed no more information. I told him that his horse was taking exception to the rear cinch of the typical Western saddle. I advised him to saddle his horse with a Western saddle at least once a week while he was at home, and to give him a good canter while loose schooling with his own two feet firmly on the ground.

Later reports from my owner suggested that his horse bucked like a professional rodeo horse with the Western saddle, but only on one occasion. He explained to me that he now rides once a week or so in the Western saddle, and his horse has been perfectly fine ever since. This was certainly one of the most memorable questions ever to come my way, and I really had to prise the information out of my owner to get to the bottom of it!

REARING

Like bucking, rearing is a very dangerous remedial problem that can only be dealt with after the horseperson reaches an appropriate level of understanding of the reasons for its existence. The information is out there, and relatively easy for horsepeople to access. One should not accept recommendations of harsh treatment to solve this or any other remedial problem.

All through my growing-up years, I watched my father hit horses on top of the head for rearing. I stood by as he advised students to do the same. Other trainers I knew advocated many procedures that I would now call criminal animal abuse. One was to drill a hole in a light bulb and fill it with warm water, and then hold it in a gloved hand. When the horse reared, the advice was to slam the light bulb on the top of his head, crushing the bulb and allowing the warm water to flow over the horse's skull. The idea was that the horse would think it was blood and stop rearing.

I remember an Irish trainer who believed that one should ride a horse at the edge of a river, encourage rearing and, when achieved, pull the horse over backwards into the river. 'It will frighten him,' he said, 'and stop him from rearing.' He advised that one should jump into the river just before the horse splashed down.

These measures seem ridiculous today, but there was a time when procedures like this were recommended consistently. The world is changing, and I am proud to be a small part of those changes. We all want it to improve faster, but we also should celebrate the progress that we are witnessing.

Question 145

I have a four-year-old piebald gelding. When I ask the horse to do something that he does not want to do, he rears. He has done this six times so far, and he has flipped over backwards twice. He fell on me once, breaking my shoulder. He understands the cues that I give him, but once he decides he would rather do something else, and I don't let him, he rears. For example, after asking for collection, he will give to

the bit, but after about ten or fifteen minutes, he will just stop and
rear. He has also reared when being driven away from the exit area of
arenas. Two separate trainers have watched me when this occurred
and informed me that this is a very dangerous behaviour that is
difficult to fix and that the best thing to do for safety's sake is to get
rid of the horse. Is this sound advice, or do you have another
suggestion?

Answer

Thank you for your inquiry. It certainly sounds as though your horse is becoming dangerous with his rearing behaviour. As you can imagine, it is difficult to diagnose the level of remedial behaviour without experiencing it: however, your question certainly describes a severe remedial problem.

The most important point to remember is that only a professional trainer and rider should deal with this behaviour. If you don't fall into this category, you need to find someone you can trust to stay safe with your horse while using non-violent techniques.

Rearing is probably the third most dangerous remedial problem a horseman can face. An in-depth knowledge of how to apply my concepts properly can keep horsepeople safe. I recommend that you read any material available regarding my concepts on the rearing horse, including my textbook. However, I can certainly discuss here the essential elements involved in re-training the horse that rears.

The first step is to eliminate any physical pain as a cause for the rearing; a high proportion of all remedial behaviour is caused by pain. Consult with the appropriate health professional and dentist in your area to diagnose and alleviate any possible pain. Once you are confident that your horse is physically comfortable and in the hands of an experienced professional trainer, you can begin to work to eliminate the behaviour. Initially, you will do Join-Up to establish a trust-based relationship, and school the horse on the Dually halter to teach him to yield to pressure.

To deal with this remedial problem, I use a piece of equipment that has been invaluable to me for over nine years, since a German racehorse taught me about this solution to a very dangerous problem. It is a type of racing blinker called a pacifier. This piece of equipment covers each eye with a screen that is similar to a tea strainer. Some horsemen tell me that when it is in place, the horse appears to have 'fly eyes'.

In addition to the pacifier, one will need a roll of duck tape. The object is to use the tape to create areas on the screen eye cover that the horse cannot see through. The underlying concept is that horses don't like to go where they can't see. This allows us to use their inherent tendency to avoid areas not clearly visible.

With the proper equipment collected, place the pacifier on the horse in the normal fashion as recommended by the manufacturer. I use this equipment for many problems, but for rearers I recommend that one tape off the top half of the goggles, so the horse can no longer see above him. Introduce the goggles over several days without a rider by working the horse loose, long lining and even leading him from another horse.

Once the horse is comfortable with the goggles, and moves in figure eights and reins back happily while working from the ground, you can start to introduce him to a 'dummy' or 'mannequin' rider. I have described in detail how to create and use this mannequin rider in my textbook. Once the horse is comfortable with the 'dummy' rider, both loose and on the long lines, a professional 'live' rider may be introduced. Initially the rider is to exert no pressure on the horse's mouth and should only sit on the horse in a relaxed fashion while the handler works the horse loose in the round pen.

The next step is to move outside the round pen with a safe saddle horse leading the way, and start asking the horse quietly to achieve more each session. The rider must take every care not to put undue pressure on the horse's mouth and to be very clear and consistent in their requests. It may be appropriate to use the Giddy-Up rope, a piece of equipment I have designed that acts as an encouragement to move forward.

If rearing is properly dealt with, however, there is no reason to throw a horse away because of this behavioural trait. It is clear that mistakes have been made in the past that have created this problem. It is just as clear that work can be done in the future that will correct it. One must, however, seek out those means that keep the people around the horse safe.

Recommended additional resource: 1

TRAIL RIDING, NERVOUS HORSES AND POTENTIAL RUNAWAYS

Trail riding is enjoyed by a vast number of people. Globally, it is growing at a rapid rate; I can't think of an activity more widely sought after in the horse business today. Many communities are mandating bridle paths as a part of their zoning regulations.

This enthusiasm for riding in the open creates its own problems. As I advise professional horsemen, I am hearing many say that a large part of their business has to do with producing horses and riders that are comfortable and safe on the trails of whatever geographical area they live and work in.

A quiet and safe horse is a sought-after commodity in the UK. It is a unique geographical area, in that most riding is done on the margins of roadways through and between towns and villages. A nervous horse that is hard to control does not provide the leisure rider with the most safe or comfortable conditions.

Question 146

I have a nine-year-old Arab–Quarter Horse cross who is a very sweet fellow, and I use your methods with him. He loves to go out on the trail, but he gets more and more excited if we go out with more than one or two other horses, and after an hour or so he is so excited and wound up that he just wants to run all the time (either that or a bone-jarring fast trot). I need help on how to calm him out on the trail. Should I get off for a little while and let him cool off? I try to stay relaxed, but after a while we are both anxious and no fun to be around. When I get him back to the barn, he is exhausted, and I am, too. I am getting my own round pen soon – would additional round-pen work help us?

Answer

Round-pen work never hurts when done properly. Causing the horse to walk, trot and canter in the round pen on a loose rein is effective therapy for the problem you have stated. Just doing round-pen work, however, is not the entire answer.

A good horseperson takes the position that at any one time one should work with small problems or small portions of big problems. The round-pen work falls into the category of a small portion of a bigger problem. One needs to make the transition from less challenging environments to more challenging environments in a logical and effective manner. This means making the transition in small steps.

The round pen is great as a beginning tool. Then obviously it is advisable to move to a slightly larger area with good footing and continue to create a quiet attitude on loose reins. Graduate from the second size to a slightly larger area and then eventually move outside any enclosure.

It is likely that your horse has galloped like the wind with other horses while in a trail-riding sort of environment. For a sensitive horse with a lot of energy this is a destructive procedure. Often horses who love to run in the first place will develop a strong desire for going fast whenever they are with other horses under these circumstances. I have seen horses that I have concluded would never be quiet trail horses after developing this habit.

If you are to be successful at correcting this behavioural pattern, you will need a great deal of patience and the cooperation of several friends and their horses, too. If you can recruit this group of horses and riders, then the method I have seen work most successfully is as follows.

Your friends agree that they will ride at a walk only. They further agree that they will ride in an area that is open enough to allow you and your horse to circle one or more of the other riders. It is further advisable that the footing be of a nature acceptable to the cantering horse.

You should allow your horse to walk on a loose rein, just as he will remember he did back in the round pen. You should not pick up the reins and tease his mouth in a fashion requesting that he go slower. Instead, leave the reins down. If your horse picks up speed, he will obviously be passing other horses. Let it happen. When approaching the front of the group, bend your horse's energy either to the left or to the right and let him trot or canter in small circles around the walking horses. You may be circling one, two or three horses, but your circle should be small so that your horse is working.

When your horse is executing these circles on a nice loose rein, ease him back to the walk near the rear of the group and allow him to walk on a loose rein with the other horses. Should your horse once again choose to increase speed, passing other horses, leave the reins down and repeat the same process, but in a circle travelling in the opposite direction to your first one.

It is important always to work horses in a balanced manner, with both left and right work in each session. This is psychologically as well as physiologically advantageous. Repeat this process until your horse is walking in a relaxed fashion or until the ride has concluded.

If you find that you have executed the entire ride with your horse failing to walk properly, I recommend that you set a date and time for the next ride and repeat the procedure. Remember that I told you that you need friends who are extremely cooperative! It is my recommendation that you make copies of this answer and distribute them among your trail-riding partners so that they too will understand the suggested plan. Once they have seen the road map, it is more likely that they will stay the course.

Question 147

What do you do with a horse that repeatedly runs to the gate?

Answer

You need to cause your horse to be uncomfortable when he is near the gate and completely comfortable when he is away from it. You can accomplish this by several means; however, I recommend cantering in small circles while near the gate. Migrate away from the gate, stop your horse, rub him and let him relax. Begin to ride again, and if he barges towards the gate, just smile and repeat the process.

You should be aware of the fact that horses that tend to run to the gate are horses that have been ridden out of the gate. As soon as a horse shows any tendency to display this undesirable behaviour, it is a good idea to refrain from riding out of the gate from that point onward. You should do your work in the training session, dismount in the centre of the enclosure and lead the horse out.

Should the horse in question continue to run to the gate, I would suggest schooling him to back out of the gate. Follow the pattern of dismounting in the centre of the work area, lead the horse in several directions, ending up at the gate, then turn the horse away from the gate and back him through the opening. I have seen this process work very well in many instances.

In the rare case where the horse continues to cause problems with this behavioural pattern even though one has followed the recommendations above, then I strongly recommend seeking other exits from the enclosure. Confuse the horse by using many gates if possible, exiting each of them under the guidelines described above. You might say, 'There's only one gate,' to which my response would be, 'Think about making another one.'

There's a short story I can tell you about Bernie, a horse I had during the time when I was involved in rodeo competitions. I used him in an event called bulldogging. I had to jump from Bernie's back on to a large steer while galloping flat out. If Bernie expected to pass through a gate on the right side of the arena, then he had a tendency to cross in front of me as I caught the steer. This action is called 'cutting you off', and generally results in a hoolahan (somersault) with seven to eight hundred pounds of steer as your tumbling partner. If Bernie anticipated leaving the arena through a gate on the left side, then he would widen from me, giving my legs a chance to handle the task without the life-threatening somersault.

The first major competition I took Bernie to was in Eugene, Oregon. As I warmed up, I recall realizing that there was no gate out of the left side of the arena. I dismounted, led Bernie to the desired area and investigated the fence line. I found a small passage where the maintenance people could go in and out. It had about a two-foot step up, after which you found yourself in the grandstand itself.

After remounting Bernie, I asked him to jump the required two feet, and then I rode him through the grandstand, down the people walk and out the back. Bernie was naughty enough to soil the grand-stands. As I left, a janitor fellow was screaming at me. I cantered away and nobody followed me with a gun.

That night, without entering the arena for any further practice or warm-up, I competed. As I leaped from Bernie's back, he made a beeline for the janitor's gate, allowing me to catch my steer in perfect shape. I was 5.2 seconds, and won the first bulldogging Bernie was used to compete with. Later that year, I was named the World Champion Intercollegiate Bulldogger, and a large part of that success was down to recognizing the needs of my horse, Bernie.

Recommended additional resource: 6

MOUTHING AND HEADSET

This is an area that has been given less attention over the past fifty years or so. I believe that it is just as important today as it was in former times. Our horses still need to learn the value of cooperating with the bit and the rider's hands.

We could categorize mouthing and creating a good headset as a lost art. In fact, it's not lost, but it certainly is an endangered species. I have, though, noticed a marked increase in interest in the creation of a good mouth and headset in recent years. It appears to me that there is hope for this all-important area to be restored to its due prominence.

Question 148

Why does my horse shake her head up and down while we are out riding?

Answer

While I am not one who quickly recommends equipment to solve problems with horses, I suggest that the use of a black iron bit with copper inlaid in the mouthpiece is often helpful with a horse that habitually tosses her head. Once you have secured the proper mouth-piece, I then recommend a process of bitting up or mouthing as outlined in my answer to Question 128 above and further described in my textbook. I believe this will help the equestrian where head tossing is concerned. It is critical for every rider to understand that the human hands are usually the culprits in creating a horse that tosses his head. As equestrians, we should always look inward before blaming the horse.

There are, in fact, several physical factors that may explain head tossing. There is a condition commonly called 'head-shaking', which is a neurological disorder. When referring to this, scientists will describe a sharp up-and-down motion like a rapid nodding of the head with the nose slightly elevated. Head-shakers are known to have a physical condition negatively affecting the Atlas joint at the base of the skull. The Atlas is the forerunner to the cervical vertebrae.

This condition is not something you can fix with bits, hands or training techniques. It is a disorder that requires medical diagnosis and attention. I have dealt with a number of head-shakers in my career and have found that there is a genetic connection. It seems that certain families tend to produce head-shakers more than others.

There is another condition that is other than a training problem and is connected with certain pollen allergies. Some horses are allergic to pollens that come into contact with the mucous membranes of the nasal passages. It seems that when the particles touch these sensitive tissues, the horse tosses his head as if there were a significant tickling deep in the nose.

To investigate the possibility of an allergy, find out if it's better to ride your horse on a certain day and/or away from cut grass/trees or certain fields. A nose net may help, and some creams make the nostrils less sensitive. Some people have found success with herbal remedies.

Rapeseed, or canola as we call it in North America, definitely produces pollen that is irritating to the breathing passages of horses. Some UK property owners have conditions in their property deeds that forbid the production of rapeseed. These properties are generally in areas where horse training is a significant activity.

One should call in a veterinarian to check if there is any potential physical problem. Once this has been accomplished, then, in the absence of a medical solution, the owner should go to work with my recommendations as to this business of head tossing.

Recommended additional resource: 1

SHY BOY

I would need a hundred pages to say all that I would like to say about this next section. Shy Boy is a wonderful member of my family now, and every day that I see him happy and healthy is a day for me to enjoy.

It is my hope that Shy Boy and I have many more years to enjoy the life that fate has carved out for us. Her Majesty Queen Elizabeth II has set me on a course with a mission to dedicate the balance of my life to the education of others in my concepts. This means that I must travel extensively, which necessitates being away from Shy Boy for long periods of time.

Nevertheless, because of his celebrity, Shy Boy gets to enjoy the visits of thousands of admirers while living in the luxury of a five-star equine facility. I believe that he is quite happy with what he perceives to be the best life possible.

Question 149

When you did Join-Up with Shy Boy in the wild, did it silence your critics? Does everyone now know that your methods work? Thanks a lot.

Answer

I would like first to ask a question myself. 'Does any one thing we ever do silence all of the critics?' The answer is '*No!*' I believe that it answered questions for many thousands of people. Many more thousands were teased into further studying the principles involved in the process they saw on video.

A percentage, however, have dismissed the whole exercise as being contrived by video presentation. In order to defend this view, they would have to believe that the BBC was acting in concert with me to cheat the public. The BBC is a large organization with a long history of leading the world in the area of creating documentaries. It had a government wildlife expert on hand as a referee. It hired the services of Dr Robert Miller, a world-renowned equine behaviourist, to observe and comment on every aspect of the exercise. The BBC brought its own film team, and they were present around the clock to watch every move that I made.

Shy Boy was wild when we started and carrying a rider when we finished, and yet some people said that he was trained before the filmed event. Others maintained that we used drugs in order to accomplish the task. Dr Miller has taken great offence at this assertion. Furthermore, any good horseperson could tell at a glance that the horse wasn't drugged.

So the answer is no; but I would estimate that at least 90 per cent of the viewers of this documentary were convinced, and many more had their heads turned in a slightly different direction. I am pleased that I did it, and I sincerely believe that Shy Boy is pleased as well.

Question 150

Do you still have Shy Boy? Where is he? I have read the Shy Boy book and seen both of the films. It seems that you took Shy Boy home, but I wasn't clear. Did you release him again or is he still a domesticated mustang? I would be interested to know what he does for activity and how his health is? I can't remember his age, but since he is a bit of a hero for me I would like to know more about his current status.

Answer

Shy Boy is at home on Flag Is Up Farms in Solvang, California. As the second DVD indicates, he came back to us and we took him home. That second DVD was made in 1998, while the first was in 1997. I have taken Shy Boy back to the wilderness several times in the past eight years and, while we have had fun out there, it seems to me he has been quite happy to return home.

The Bureau of Land Management (BLM) records show that he was born in 1994 and captured in 1997 near Tonopah, Nevada.

He is a wonderful little horse who loves people and especially children. Thank you for asking about him, as it gives me a chance to let everyone know that he is happy and fine. Shy Boy is active in the training programme here at Flag Is Up. He often escorts young

Thoroughbreds to and from the racetrack and even assists them in learning about the starting gate and other procedures that tend to frighten young race prospects. Occasionally Shy Boy will be asked to assist the young Western cutting horses that are in training and seems to have a lot of fun with this activity.

In the recent past, Shy Boy was even ridden by a young lady who was interested in dressage. While he will never be a competitive dressage horse, he did learn to move in a very attractive fashion under the dressage saddle and did not appear to be out of place, even in this discipline well removed from anything to which he was accustomed.

Many of Shy Boy's fans will remember that he travelled extensively in the Western part of the United States during the late 1990s and early 2000s. He was a presence at a public television broadcasting studio while they aired his DVDs as part of a PBS fundraiser. He was perfectly comfortable going into studios with lights, cameras and many objects that would frighten an ordinary horse.

Literally hundreds of millions of people (one million on site and the rest by TV) watched Shy Boy lead five other mustangs down Colorado Boulevard in the 2004 and 2005 Tournament of Roses Parade in Pasadena, California on New Year's Day. He was a role model for the other horses, and a perfect mount for my wife, Pat, who led our mustang contingency while riding this wonderful partner of ours.

At age thirteen, Shy Boy looks terrific, and to observe him at home on Flag Is Up you would get the impression that he feels he owns the place and all the other horses residing here are simply meant to keep him company. Some nice people donated a special floor (Comfort Stall) for Shy Boy's stall. It is a cushy rubber mat and with the bedding over it, it's as though he's on a cloud. His days are spent either working or in an outside paddock, and at night he's on his cloud. On our front gate it says 'Visitors Welcome', and we mean it. You can come and see Shy Boy any time you want.

Recommended additional resources: 6, 10

CONCLUSION

On behalf of horses everywhere, I would like to thank not only those who asked questions of me that made it into this book, but everyone who has asked questions of me throughout my career. There were literally hundreds of thousands of them. Each one teased some section of my brain, encouraging it to come up with an answer, and then there were more questions. If the answers weren't there, I felt compelled to work harder to seek them out.

High among my goals for this book is to find that readers have accepted my answers not as a pill or certain cure, but as encouragement towards a mindset that allows for natural communication with horses. To come to an understanding of the needs of these animals that give us so much, we need to communicate rather than to dominate.

It is the next generation to whom we owe these answers. Subsequent to my discoveries, it is my hope that they will no longer accept traditional horsemanship if it includes violence and force. I pray that they will continue to ask the hard questions and demand logical answers that meet the needs of the horses we cherish.

My hope is that young people will continue to send me questions and to bring them in person to my events as well. I encourage you to send questions through to my website, to my newsletter, and even through the certified instructors that I have out there working hard to educate people in my concepts throughout the world.

Another goal I have for this book is not to have answered all of the questions, but to create more questions within the minds of horsepeople everywhere. It is clear that no one person possesses all of the questions and even far clearer that no one has all of the answers.

Perhaps in the next ten years I will receive another generation of questions from which to create another book, and perhaps there is a young horseperson out there somewhere who by that time will be able to answer them better than I can. Advancement in our relationship with horses is moving far more rapidly than in our relationships with one another. I believe that horses could teach our world leaders a few things about how we could get along better with each other.

Thanks to the movement that has taken the violence out of the science of training horses, we have rapidly become much better at communicating in *Equus*. I dedicate this book to become a stepping-stone to reaching my life's goal, which is to leave the world a better place than I found it – for horses, and for people, too.

RECOMMENDED ADDITIONAL RESOURCES

1   *From My Hands to Yours: Lessons from a Lifetime of Training Championship Horses.* This is Monty's textbook, including the very first 'Dictionary of *Equus*', clearly depicting the signs and reciprocal gestures between human and equine through photos and illustrations. *From My Hands to Yours* shares Monty's Join-Up® horse-training methods with you, both on the ground and under saddle.

You'll learn to work with remedial behaviour in your horse such as biting, pulling back, rearing and bucking.

Basic movements such as stopping, turning and changing leads are also included.

Monty's methods are meticulously described so you can apply his hard-earned knowledge to your own training experiences.

2   *Horse Sense for People*: In this book Monty asks us to rethink the way we use power over others and shows you how with people, as with horses, the gentle way is the better way. Practical, philosophical and provocative, *Horse Sense for People* demonstrates how trust, respect and communication – not coercion – are the keys to fruitful relationships.

This book is rich in anecdotes about both horses and people; it applies the lifetime of lessons Monty has learned from horses to the way we relate to each other in the workplace and at home. These metaphors illustrate a new way of seeing and experiencing your relationships.

For example, Monty tells the story of the wild mustang mare that connected with him so quickly that she protected him from what she perceived to be a terrible threat. Monty guides us to understand and empathize with his stories and to transfer this learning to more effective human communication.

3   *Join-Up* DVD: Join-Up® is a consistent set of training principles using the horse's inherent methods of communication and herd behaviour rather than force. The result is a willing partnership in

which the horse's performance can flourish to its full potential, rather than exist within the boundaries of obedience.

In this film, Monty discusses the foundation of Join-Up and the philosophy behind it all. This is a great introduction to the basic principles that Monty uses in all his work.

4 *The Man Who Listens to Horses*: This is the revolutionary number one best seller that started it all! *The Man Who Listens to Horses* spent more than a year on the *New York Times* best-seller list, sold more than 4.6 million copies worldwide, and was hailed by the *San Francisco Chronicle* as 'the kind of life-altering book you never want to finish'. Monty shares his extraordinary life and what led him to develop a gentle, more effective method of working with horses in a language they could understand – their own.

5 *Dually*™ DVD: This educational DVD accompanies the Dually Training Halter designed by Monty: a patented schooling halter, which effectively rewards horses for acting in partnership with the handler. This useful training aid will help get the most out of your work when leading, loading and long-lining, when used as a bitless bridle and in many more ways.

6 *The Horses in My Life*: a celebration of the horses from whom Monty has learned the most, as well as those that have impressed themselves most indelibly on his memory and in his heart. All the horses featured inside – from his first horse Ginger to world-famous Thoroughbreds and the American mustang Shy Boy, the star of the often-repeated PBS documentary and best-selling book *Shy Boy* – have contributed something unique to Monty's understanding of their kind. He pictures each as a stone on a necklace, adding them one by one, allowing you to relish his stories of great warmth and affection. Monty never lost sight of how much each horse meant to him, and *The Horses in My Life* is his tribute to their memory.

7 *Fix-Up* DVD: The Fix-Up series takes Join-Up training principles

and applies them to common remedial problems such as crossing water, head-shy horses, pulling back when tied, fearing the veterinarian, trailer loading, mounting issues, kicking and preparing for the farrier. Monty walks you through each challenging behaviour, showing you how the horse's instincts affect its actions – and how to use this same instinctual behaviour to train your horse for these challenges.

8 *Follow-Up* DVD: Join Monty as he guides two unstarted horses through their first four days of Join-Up®. This DVD provides an in-depth description of how to train unstarted horses humanely using their instinctual behaviour for better results.

9 *Load-Up* DVD: Gain valuable insight while watching Monty use both a step-up and a ramp trailer while dealing with a Thoroughbred filly who has a deep-seated fear of loading. You'll be amazed at how horses can learn to load into the trailer so freely.

10 *Shy Boy* DVD: This film continues the story of the little wild mustang that Monty adopted from the Bureau of Land Management and featured as the subject of the PBS documentary *A Real Horse Whisperer*. You will fall in love with Shy Boy, now America's most famous mustang horse.

11 *Perfect Match* DVD: Whether you are buying your first horse or have owned a number of horses, this educational DVD will help you avoid the common pitfalls that even experienced professionals encounter when acquiring a horse.

12 *Rosie* DVD: In this educational DVD, you can observe Monty working with a wild mustang at her own pace without causing her to experience pain or force. Watch as Monty is asked to find creative solutions to the difficult questions asked by this challenging and raw young mare. Rosie, an ultra-sensitive adopted mustang from the Bureau of Land Management, is following Monty around less than six

minutes into her first lesson. Then the fun begins, as she demands Monty's full capabilities to help her learn to carry a human rider safely. Plastic bags, telescoping de-sensitizers and dummy riders are tools Monty employs with patience and common sense to help Rosie move through this traditionally traumatic process with trust and confidence.

13 *You and Your Wild Horse* DVD: This set of films gives you the tools to train your wild horse using Monty's consistent set of principles called Join-Up. You will learn how to create a low-cost environment that will assist in educating your wild horse safely and effectively. This educational DVD documents Monty going through each step of the process with a real Bureau of Land Management wild horse, from the moment he steps off the trailer to his first ride on a trail. Whether yours is an adopted horse or domestic but completely unhandled, these principles will get you both safely on the trail.

14 *Gentling Your Spooky Horse* DVD: Watch Monty and a student use desensitization to teach a horse to accept such potential 'predators' as plastic bags and balloons. Have more fun with your horse by enjoying routines that take your horse from wild and spooky to relaxed and happy.

15 **Monty Roberts International Learning Center**: The Monty Roberts International Learning Center is part of the non-profit organization Join-Up International Inc., dedicated to promoting gentle, more effective alternatives to violence and force. Monty Roberts, Dean of Students, leads a team of exceptional certified instructors who have dedicated themselves to sharing Monty's training philosophies by completing an extensive certification process.

The Monty Roberts International Learning Center is unique among training facilities because the primary focus of the curriculum is on equine psychology and behaviour rather than riding skills. Students develop a solid understanding of what motivates and influences equine behaviour in order to increase their effectiveness in the application of their choice: virtually any discipline of riding, veterinary assistance, shoeing, racehorse training and so forth.

The Monty Roberts International Learning Center is located at Flag Is Up Farms in the Santa Ynez Valley, California, just forty miles north of Santa Barbara. Visitors are welcomed between 9 a.m. and 5 p.m. daily, free of charge.

16 *Join-Up Journal*: Monty Roberts' *Join-Up Journal*™ offers ideas from the most sensitive minds in the horse industry and shares inspirational thoughts from the most learned equine sources. The *Join-Up Journal* provides information that will assist you on the path to force-free training and encourage you to bring understanding and trust to your horses, family members and others.

FOR MORE INFORMATION

My life's goal is to leave the world a better place than I found it, for horses and for people, too.

In pursuit of that end, I invite you to call or go online for further information regarding the Monty Roberts International Learning Center, clinics, conferences, educational DVDs or videos and other educational material, including my published books:

The Man Who Listens to Horses
Shy Boy: The Horse That Came in from the Wild
Join-Up
Horse Sense for People
From My Hands to Yours: Lessons from a Lifetime of Training
  Championship Horses
The Horses in My Life

USA toll-free phone number:
1-888-U2-MONTY (1-888-826-6689)

From outside the United States:
00 1 805 688 6288 or 00 1 805 688 4382

Fax: 00 1 805 688 2242 or 00 1 805 688 9709

Websites: www.montyroberts.com and www.montyroberts.co.uk
General e-mail: admin@montyroberts.com

Newsletter to submit questions to Monty:
newsletter@montyroberts.com

INDEX

Page references in italics denote that the question is illustrated.

C

canter 62–4, 79–80, 89, 184

castration 49, 136

catching a horse 17–18

cattle
  fear of 96, *103–5*
  working 67–8, 176

chambons 217

changing legs 61–4

chestnut horses 60, 61

child abuse 21, 23

children, working with 20–21

chondroitin 133, 150

choosing a horse 152–4

cinch-bound horses 203–5

clicking sound, response to 42–4

clippers, fear of *95–6*

Co-enzymeQ10 134, 141, 181

colostrum 146, 182

colour-blindness 22

colour of skin and sensitivity 59–61

communication 47, 69–70, 157–8, 211
  gestures 33–6, 69, 77, 89
  see also Equus; Join-Up

competition
  gaited horses 164
  reining horses 177–8
  rider anxiety 9–11
  show jumpers 172–4

and stallions 50
  Western division 176–7

controversial, accusation of being
  18–20

cow work 67–8, 176

cows, fear of 96, *103–5*

cribbing 233–4

cutting horses 67–8

D

D-shaped enclosure *115–16*

dangerous behaviour
  bucking 235–7
  kicking *222–5*
  rearing 238–41

dark-skinned horses 59–60

de-bonding process 111

de-sensitizing
  strong smells 109
  using hairdryer 95–6

deer 35–6, 45

demonstrations 179

diaphragmatic breathing 11–14

diet 136–8, 151

discipline 20–21, 50–51, 78–9

Dog Listener, The (Fennell) 163

dogs 107, 163

donkeys 161

draw reins 216–17

dreaming 56–7
dressage 70, 141–2, 173–4
du Pont, Camilla 174
Dually halter 40–2, 195, 225, 227–8
dummy rider 240

E
early training 57–9
ears
 pinned back 44
 touching 207–9
education 7–8, 157–8, 180
elastic over-girth 204
elderly horses 148–51
elderly riders 152–3
electric fence 54
emotion 66
emotional conflict 124
enclosures *81*, 83–4, 210–12, 242–3
'end of the day' reward 71
English saddle 236
entire male horses 49, 136
entry level 152–6, 158
equipment
 bits 206–7, 217–20, 225, 247
 chambons 217
 draw reins 216–17
 Dually halter *40–42*, 195, 225, 227–8
 Giddy-Up rope 70, 140

kicking rings *222–5*
long lines 220–21
martingales 215–16
pocketknife 231
rug 228–30
saddles 155, 203–5, 213–14, 236–7
side pull 225
side reins *221–2*
Equus 22–3, 33–8, 72, 84, 210
evolutionary development 39
exercise saddle 213–14
exercise, stretching 141–2
exhaustion 89
extra-old horses 148–51
extrinsic learning 26–8
eye movements 35–6

F
fainting, when watching Join-Up 23–4
farrier, preparing horse for 128–30
fears and phobias 90–92
 animals 96–7
 auditory 97–8
 birds 96–7
 bridges 99
 clippers *95–6*
 cows *103–5*
 plastic bags 92–4
 tarpaulins *101–2*

dreaming 56–7
grieving 46
imprinting 58, 143–7
movement 61–4
sensitivity 59–61
social order 44–6, 53–4
sound, response to 42–4
stubbornness 40–42, 162
tail swishing 68–70
territorial attitude 44
trust 28–9, 33, 47, 48, 123, 208
yawning 55
pulling back 114–18
pulse rate 11, 12, 14
punishment 14–16, 78–9

Q

quality of life 148
quality time 80, 111, 149–50
Quarter Horse 138, 189, 219
Queen Elizabeth II 61, 88, 179–80, 249

R

racehorses 201–2, 215
   lameness 139
racing blinkers 240
racing mules 162
range of motion 132–3
rapeseed 248

re-oxygenating the brain 55
rearing 238–41
refusal to jump 172–3
regulations and guidelines 165
reining horses 177–8
relationship with horses 25, 78–9
relaxation 48, 89, 200
   of horseman 12, 14
remedial grooming 201–2
remedial horses and Join-Up 82–3
remedial problems
   bucking 235–7
   loading 27, 192–200
   rearing 238–41
   separation anxiety 110–13
Rescue Cream 140
Rescue Remedy 49, 140
resentment 32, 69
retirement 149
*Revolution in Horsemanship and What it
   Means to Mankind* (Miller and
   Lamb) 85
reward 50–52, 71, 188
rider anxiety 9–11
riding bareback 154–5
riding competitions 24–5
riding schools 30–32
Rocky Mountain Horse 153, 164
rodeo competitions 245–6

stallions 47, 49–50, 135–6, 149

standing martingale (tie-down) 215, 216

standing still 225–8

starting 72, 79–80, 85–7

stewardship 148–9

stopping at a fence 172–3

stress 10, 49

stretching exercises 141–2

stroking 52

strong smells, de-sensitizing 109

stubbornness 40–42, 162

stumbling 132–3, 149

swinging 125–6

swish-tail horses 68–70

synchronicity 12

T

tail swishing 68–70

taking the bit 206–7

talking to horses 36, 37–8

tarpaulin 101–2, 229

teaching 27

Tennessee Walking Horse 74–5, 153, 165, 166–7

territorial attitude 44

tetherballs 233

therapy animals 159

Thoroughbreds 74, 120–3, 213

   grooming 201–2

three-beat gait 62–4

Tina 161, 162

tiring 55

tolt 153, 165

touching 51–2

toys 232–3

traditional training methods 14–17, 19, 82–3

trail riding 167, 242–4

trailers

   backing out of 197–200

   buying 191–2

   flying out of backwards 196–200

   loading 27–8, 94, 192–5, 197–200

   tying horse in 117–18, 195–6

   types 191–2

training 28–9, 48–9

   frightening objects, use of 126

   patience 25–6

   recognizing progress 25–6

   traditional methods 14–17, 19, 82–3

   unresponsive to 59

   violence-free 15–16, 20–22, 25–6, 47

Transfer Factor™ 133–4, 140, 181, 182

transportation *see* trailers

travelling and visits 179–81

trees, walking under 102–3

trot 62

trust 28–9, 33, 47, 48, 123, 208

INDEX   273

turnout rug 228–30

tying horse in trailer 117–18, 195–6

NOTES

The rest of the pages are intentionally blank so you may use the space for your own notes.

NOTES

NOTES

NOTES

ASK MONTY • MONTY ROBERTS

NOTES

NOTES